Editing Fact and Fiction

Editing Fact and Fiction is a concise, practical guide for people interested in book publishing or already working as editors who want to learn more about the opportunities in various kinds of book editing. Writing in a lively, informal style, two editors with extensive experience in a wide variety of fields—fiction and nonfiction, trade and reference, academic and commercial publishing—explain what editors in different jobs really do. They discuss the rewards and limitations of editing for different kinds of publishers and list the personal qualities that will equip editors to meet the demands of their jobs.

Editing Fact and Fiction takes the reader step by step through the editing process, from manuscript to bound book. It discusses the principles of sound editing and provides many specific examples of how to—and how not to—edit copy. It gives advice on how to deal tactfully with authors and cites examples of when editorial restraint is the best intervention. Finally, it includes a guide to editorial freelancing, a chapter on the use of computers, and an extensive listing of publishing courses.

Editing
Fact and Fiction

A Concise Guide to Book Editing

LESLIE T. SHARPE   IRENE GUNTHER

CAMBRIDGE
UNIVERSITY PRESS

Published by the Press Syndicate of the University of Cambridge
The Pitt Building, Trumpington Street, Cambridge CB2 1RP
40 West 20th Street, New York, NY 10011-4211, USA
10 Stamford Road, Oakleigh, Melbourne 3166, Australia

First published 1994

Printed in the United States of America

Library of Congress Cataloging-in-Publication Data
Sharpe, Leslie T.
Editing fact and fiction : a concise guide to book editing /
Leslie T. Sharpe, Irene Gunther.
p. cm.
Includes bibliographical references and index.
ISBN 0-521-45080-2. — ISBN 0-521-45693-2 (pbk.)
1. Editing. I. Gunther, Irene. II. Title.
PN162.S4435 1994 94-2334
808'.02—dc20 CIP

A catalog record for this book is available from the British Library.

ISBN 0-521-45080-2 hardback
ISBN 0-521-45693-2 paperback

Contents

Contents

Acknowledgments

Many people contributed to this book, sharing editing experience and insights with us and giving generously of their time. In particular, we wish to thank Barbara Birmingham, Louise Bloomfield, Sheila Buff, David Burr, Rosemary Brosnan, Virginia Buckley, Elaine Chubb, Judy Davis, Robert Famighetti, Tracy Farrell, Inez Glucksman, Patricia Godfrey, Lynn Goldberg, Erika Goldman, Carmen Gomez, Joellyn Goodman, Lisa Healy, Nancy Jackson, Bernard Johnston, Rebecca Koh, Judy Levey, Laurie Lewis, Carolyn Marino, Anita Mondello, Trumbull Rogers, John Smallwood, Carolyn Smith, Norah Vincent, and Robert Weil.

We are especially grateful to Beth Luey, whose careful review and thoughtful suggestions helped make this a better book. At Cambridge University Press, special thanks go to our editor, Sidney Landau, for his support, open-mindedness, and commitment to our book; to Eric Newman, our eagle-eyed copyeditor; and to Nancy Feldman, for help along the way. Thanks also to our agent, Elizabeth Backman, an editor at heart, who believed in this project.

Irene Gunther wishes to thank Milton Horowitz, a long-time mentor, who started her on the road to becoming an editor. And she thanks her sons, Marc, Noel, and Andrew Gunther, for their unfailing support and encouragement.

Leslie T. Sharpe wishes to thank Michael di Capua, who set for her the highest standard of editing excellence. And she especially thanks Hannah Sharpe, the best patron—and press agent—a writer could have.

a predecessor of mine as editor-in-chief at The Dial Press, once sent an editorial letter to an author in which he re-wrote one of the author's paragraphs to show her how much better it could be. I haven't read the book in question, but I have a vision of that paragraph standing out like a search-light on a dark street, a passage by a fine writer in a work of vastly different style. I think Doctorow made a mistake—the author would have been better served if she had been made to put that paragraph in her own words, her own voice.

Readers of this book will not make such a mistake. They will know how to start and where to stop. They will learn patience, tact, respect, and love, not only for the writer but for his language as well, and for the amazing, infuriating process called publishing.

And maybe this blessed profession can pick itself up by its paragraphs, and care about books again.

Yes, the authors have given us each nut and every bolt ("*cliché!*" screams the editor) of the editorial process. But they've given us something far more valuable. Through all the chapters of this book shines a love of words, of *good English*, so lacking in publishing today.

For the craft of acquiring good writing is a disappearing one. "Bring us big books," proclaim the heads of the publishing conglomerates. "Big books by 'big' authors." By this they mean books that will make money; if they'd wanted to say *good* books, they'd have done so. And the promising writer, the careful, subtle user of symbol and metaphor, the elegant stylist, is in danger of no longer being published.

Copyediting, too, is in decline. Since "big" books are expensive, and the publishing houses have to recoup the money they've laid out as quickly as possible, "good" schedules (meaning short schedules) are more important than good English. Indeed, the sentence I quoted at the beginning of this foreword had no effect on the sale of the book, though I pleaded with a friend to boycott the novel.

We are in an age of what E. L. Doctorow called "network publishing" (it's no surprise that most of the conglomerates have television or movie arms) where what matters is money, not craft.

Well, this is a book about *craft*, and if it instills in the reader a realization that language and style and care are important, that phrasing and organization and clarity *count*, it will have accomplished a great measure of its larger purpose.

It has another larger purpose, too, in my opinion, beautifully laid out in Chapters 4 and 5: the understanding that an editor's job is not to *change* a book, but to bring out the author's voice in the strongest way possible. A book belongs to the author, not the editor; the editor's job is to lay an objective eye on what is fundamentally subjective work (even if it's a book on knitting) so that if the author is careless or fuzzy or just carried away by his own enthusiasm, the editor can catch him up on it.

In other words, the editor should not rewrite but rather tell the author to rewrite, and why. The same Mr. Doctorow,

Foreword

by Richard Marek

"The General made an audible noise."

I read this sentence in a bestseller recently, and it made my editor's blood boil. Go try and make an *inaudible* noise, damn it, I wanted to yell. Where was the editor for this novel? The copyeditor? The proofreader?

You'll read about redundancy in this book, as you'll read about innumerable other sins that authors make and editors should catch. You'll find out, too, about the variety of tasks, despite considerable overlapping, among an acquisitions editor, a managing editor, a copyeditor, and a proofreader. You'll discover the marked differences between an editor for a commercial trade house and one who works on textbooks. You'll get to know the full range of what every editor does, presented with wit, verve, completeness, tact, and passion.

Leslie T. Sharpe and Irene Gunther have written by far the most complete manual for editors ever published, and they've spiced it with dozens of examples, taken from life, that will delight everyone who has had or is about to have a career in publishing.

Richard Marek has been in publishing for over thirty years. He was an editor at Macmillan, a senior editor at World, editor-in-chief at The Dial Press, had his own imprint at Putnam and then St. Martin's, was president and publisher of E. P. Dutton, became editor-at-large at Crown, and now is president of his own company, Marek & Charles, which provides editorial, design, and manufacturing services.

Among the authors he has edited are James Baldwin, Robert Ludlum, Thomas Harris, Aaron Copland, and a twelve-year-old girl named Latoya Hunter.

Introduction

Editing Fact and Fiction is a hands-on guide to book editing. The senior editor will find it useful for its sources and as a training manual for apprentice editors; copyeditors and proofreaders can use it as a refresher course; and for the would-be editor—recent college graduates or someone contemplating a career change—it is a primer of contemporary publishing and editing practices.

Editing is a broad-ranging concept, an art as well as a craft. In crossword puzzles, the word "edit" is the answer to a whole list of clues: review, revise, alter, redact, refine, emend, correct. The craft can be learned fairly easily by diligent attention to the rules of grammar and the conventions of usage and style. To master the art, however, rules are not enough; this mastery requires a special sensibility, a finely tuned ear, and an instinct that comes only with years of experience.

A Good Editor Is Hard to Find

Our basic premise is that every book—whether it's a literary masterpiece, a physics textbook, or a sci-fi novel—deserves the attention of an editor who knows his or her stuff. By "editing," we mean the art and craft of shaping and refining a manuscript into a publishable book.

But good editing takes time. Unfortunately, in today's publishing environment editors have little time to learn how to edit and even less to do it well. For many senior editors, reading manuscripts and editing the chosen few is a task that must be left to evenings and weekends. An editor's day is likely to be consumed by telephone calls, staff meetings, writer conferences, contract negotiations, and correspondence, as well as by the myriad production decisions each book demands. The late, great editor Henry Robbins once lamented, "What I need is an extra set of eyes, another pair of hands, and a forty-eight-hour day."

An overworked editor can't edit effectively. More than a decade ago, *Time* magazine deplored "The Decline of Editing" (September 1, 1980), citing an alarming increase in errors and stylistic infelicities. The book editors and publishers interviewed generally blamed editing's fall from grace on too many books being published and too little time for editors to deal adequately with each.

Low salaries have also taken a toll, discouraging highly qualified candidates from entering the field. Editors of every stripe are routinely paid less than their colleagues in marketing, sales, and subsidiary rights. This is consistent with the outworn but lingering image of editing as a "gentleman's profession." Historically, publishing was a business that was supposedly above business. Editors, in particular, had a genteel, ivory-tower aura, and money was assumed to be beneath them.

Today, no one would contest that publishing is a business. The change began after World War II with the publication of the first mass-market paperbacks and accelerated in the 1960s, when public demand for cheaper editions led to the paperback revolution. More recently, publishing went through another "revolution," as smaller houses were swallowed up by larger ones. In turn, some bigger publishers were taken over, becoming part of huge conglomerates. One result of this trend is a greater emphasis on profits. Another is that the small, independent publisher has become an endangered species.

But publishing's focus on profits has not been reflected in editors' paychecks. "I think there's a theory in publishing that editing is, if not counterproductive, at least not as productive as hustling," says James D. Landis, William Morrow's former president and editorial director. "You're not going to make money editing the way you will make money discovering someone who needs to be edited."[1]

For editors, "hustling"—namely, buying books they think will sell—has of necessity become the first order of business. Promotions are more likely to come from discovering top-selling talent than from doing a talented editing job.

Symptomatic of the devaluing of editing is the fact that today it is increasingly assigned to outside contractors. Publishers have traditionally farmed out production tasks such as typesetting and printing; but until recently they kept editing for themselves, considering it intrinsic to the quality of a book. Now many composition (typesetting) houses, and even some printers, routinely offer editorial services. And packagers—small firms with low overhead costs who put together books for publishers—stand ready to handle almost every phase of book production. They will develop an idea for a book or for a series, acquire authors and illustrators, edit the manuscript, supervise the typesetting, and deliver a final product ready to go to the printer.

Still, it would be a mistake to assume that publishers, even the admittedly commercial ones, are engaged in a conspiracy to sabotage literature or to eradicate good writing. Any editor is delighted to discover a manuscript that is both salable and well written. "Unfortunately," says longtime literary agent and writer Richard Curtis, "a well-written book may be just as unsalable as a poorly written one; it just breaks your heart a little more to return it to the author."[2]

Nor should editing's decline be blamed solely on economic factors. Skilled copyeditors, long the mainstay of any editorial department, are a vanishing breed. Copy chiefs quoted in a *New York Times* article (March 13, 1990) attributed this

[1] Gerald Gross, ed., *Editors on Editing*, rev. ed. New York: Harper & Row, 1983, pp. 104–05.
[2] Richard Curtis, *How to Be Your Own Literary Agent*. Boston: Houghton Mifflin, 1983, p. 2.

to schools that neglect English and history, as well as to a money-saving trend toward using freelancers (whose skills can vary widely) rather than keeping copyeditors on staff. The result, they said, is more errors in books.

A general deterioration in the quality of writing has also made editing more difficult. Every author has a horror story about a copyeditor's egregious mistakes; every copyeditor can match it with one of her own about an author's abysmal prose.

Poor writing has even induced some literary agents to become editors themselves, working on manuscripts before submitting them to publishers. It has also contributed to the emergence of a new entrepreneur. For a fee, the "literary consultant" will advise a writer on a manuscript's merit *before* the writer sends it to an agent.

The "Un" Professional Profession

According to *Merriam-Webster's Collegiate Dictionary* (10th edition), a profession is "a calling requiring specialized knowledge and often long and intensive academic preparation." Editors think of themselves—and are considered by others—as members of a profession. But does editing meet the definition?

There are no postgraduate degrees in editing[3] and, unlike professions such as law, medicine, or accounting, no qualifying examinations.[4] Indeed, editing is as "unprofessionalized" as it was in the days when publishing was a "gentlemanly" pursuit. By this we mean that at most houses, editors are simply not taught how to edit; it is just assumed

[3] See Chapter 8 for a listing of the editing and publishing-related courses and programs offered by universities and editing organizations, some for undergraduate credit or certification.

[4] The Board of Editors in the Life Sciences has developed a process for testing and evaluating proficiency in editing in the life sciences. (For information, contact Board of Editors in the Life Sciences [BELS], P.O. Box 824, Highlands, NC 28741–0824.) But there is no such process established for editing overall.

that they know how or else will pick it up as they go along.

Furthermore, whatever training is given editors is not standardized industrywide. Even at the same house, editorial instruction can vary greatly, depending on the editor to whom the newcomer is apprenticed.

How, then, do editors acquire the "specialized knowledge" necessary for their craft? Mostly the hard way. The editorial assistant who finally gets her first manuscript to edit is apt to find the experience intimidating. Typically, everyone around her will be too busy to take her by the hand and lead her through the intricacies of editing. She will probably be given a copy of the house style rules and a few general instructions about that particular book and left to "get on with it." For the rest, she'll have to rely on her own instincts and education.

A Principled Approach

It's true that most new employees, whatever their field, have to learn as best they can on the job. It's equally true that, given the demands of the editing profession, new editors would be greatly helped if they had a set of basic principles to guide them.

This book offers such a set of principles, which are designed to facilitate the tasks of beginners and experienced editors alike. Introduced and illustrated with practical examples in Chapter 3, they constitute an underpinning for the whole book, from the nitty-gritty advice we offer on copyediting (see, in particular, Chapter 4) to the discussion of the editor's sensibility and the author/editor relationship in Chapter 5.

The principles will eliminate the trial-and-error approach to editing by giving beginners the tools they need to tackle a manuscript with confidence—and to make the hundreds of little judgments the job demands.

And senior editors can use the principles to train junior staff members and start them along the path toward becoming editing professionals. We believe this approach would substantially reduce the time required for editors to learn their job and thus translate into cost savings for publishers.

Editing from Our Experience

Both authors have spent the better part of their working lives working with words—their own and other people's. Our joint editing experience is varied as well as extensive. Between us, we have edited commercial and literary fiction, nonfiction, poetry, children's books, textbooks, and reference works. We have worked in-house and as freelancers and have hired and trained freelancers and staff. In addition, Leslie T. Sharpe has led workshops and taught courses in editing and creative writing; Irene Gunther has worked as senior editor in the reference division of a major publishing house and, previous to that, as editorial director, supervising all stages of the editing and production of college textbooks.

We are both also widely published writers. Irene Gunther is the author of a well-received young adult biography; she has also contributed articles to major newspapers and magazines. Leslie T. Sharpe's articles and essays have appeared in many national magazines and newspapers.

As editors, both of us are self-taught. We began with a love of words and learned as we went: from our own mistakes, from other's helping hands, from exposure to fine editing, and perhaps most of all from a constant contact with books and manuscripts. We also learned from style manuals and editing texts, of which there are many. What we missed was a handy, concise guide to the basics of book editing.

Editing Fact and Fiction is that guide. It is also a useful sourcebook for editors in every area of publishing, providing an annotated bibliography, telephone reference sources and hotlines, lists of publishing course offerings, and lists of professional organizations.

Introduction

We wrote the book as editors, for editors; as writers, we stress the consideration due writers and writing. That "consideration" was occasionally tested in our own collaboration—a fully equal one, to which each of us brought our particular writing skills and editing expertise—as we critically evaluated each other's ideas and appraised each other's prose. Along the way, we were reminded of how frustrating editing can be—and also how rewarding it is.

There are few things as satisfying as making a book its best possible self. That is the editor's challenge. Ours is to help editors reach that goal.

Chapter 1

Who (and What) Is an Editor?

To many people embarking on a career, as well as to those in the general public with a love of books and reading, publishing has a special mystique. And the job of editor is held in high prestige.

It is also cloaked in mystery. What is an editor? What does he or she do? Even publishing insiders find it hard to answer those questions because the title "editor" is a catch-all that includes a multitude of jobs and functions. Acquiring editor, managing editor, line editor, copyeditor, production editor—these are just a few of the confusing species.

What do those who share the title of editor have in common? What distinguishes one from the other? The simple answer is that all of them deal with words, but they do so in different ways and to varying degrees. Some editors deal with broad concepts, others see to it that commas and hyphens are in the right place, still others are concerned with how the words will appear on the printed page. Let us go into an editorial department and take a closer look at some of the species.

Classifying the Species

Acquiring Editor

The *acquiring editor* is the person most people have in mind when they hear the word "editor." (He or she is also known as *senior acquisitions, general,* or *senior* editor or, if the head of a department, as *editorial director.* For the sake of simplicity, we will refer to this editor either as acquiring or senior editor.)

The life of a book begins with the acquiring editor; it is she who sets in motion the long and often arduous process that turns a stack of typewritten pages, a computer printout, or just an idea scribbled on a sheet of paper into a bound book.

The acquiring editor is the closest thing to an entrepreneur in publishing. As her title implies, her most important function is buying books. She goes about this in many ways and uses many different sources. Some books are submitted to her by literary agents, others by writers she has already published; some books she originates herself by suggesting ideas to writers or to their agents; still others are acquired at auctions, where she bids against other publishers for a "hot" project she would like to have for her house. (Auctions, in which bids are placed over the phone, are generally originated by agents trying to get the best possible price for a new manuscript or, more commonly, for the paperback edition of a bestselling hardcover book.) Occasionally, she will take a book by an unknown author that has come in "over the transom," meaning that it was unsolicited (although, according to editors we spoke to, nowadays this happens more and more rarely).

Finding books is an active and ongoing process. A good editor does not sit back and wait for projects to come her way—in the office and outside it, she is constantly on the lookout for ideas; she talks with agents, often wining and dining them; she browses through bookstores, reads newspapers and magazines; she may get the germ of an idea by listening to the radio, watching television, or chatting with friends; she always has one eye on the market and one on what other publishers are doing.

Once she has found a manuscript she wants to publish, she becomes a seller rather than a buyer, the author's advocate, and the promoter of the book-to-be. Her first step is to "sell" the book to the people inside her house, which generally happens at an editorial meeting.

In order to be convincing to her colleagues and her boss, the senior editor has to do her homework. She must come well prepared to the meeting, at which people from sales and marketing as well as other editors (usually including the editorial director and sometimes the publisher) will be present. "In today's competitive market," says the editorial director of a children's book department, "it is no longer enough to announce that this is a well-written book and I love it. You have to work up the facts and figures on every aspect: size and cost, photos and illustrations, projected sales and marketing plans, and, of course, the competition. Ideally, you try to find a marketing handle. For example, I recently bought a book about a group of Salvadoran children who were smuggled into the United States. It worked because it was a good story. It also helped that it had a multicultural handle."

In nonfiction, particularly, the author's qualifications to write the book must be credible. And—sad to say—the way the author will come across in TV interviews is sometimes taken into consideration.

In practice, most senior editors have a lot of leeway in choosing their books. To have reached their present position in the publishing house, they must have already convinced their superiors of their judgment and taste. Although an occasional project (perhaps one that requires a large up-front investment) may be turned down, the senior editor will generally be able to persuade her colleagues that the book she is promoting to them is worth publishing.

After the book has been accepted, the senior editor negotiates the terms of the contract with the author or, more often, the author's agent. These include the amount of the royalties (the percentage the author is to receive from the sale of each copy), the size of the advance (the money paid up front to the author in anticipation of future sales) and when it will be paid, the delivery date(s) of the manuscript (some manuscripts are delivered in batches), as well as other matters such as subsidiary rights, which include the right to sell the book to another publisher, for example, for a mass-market edition, foreign rights, magazine and newspaper rights, and movie and television rights.

As the book is being produced, the senior editor continues to sell it in various ways. She pitches it at the company's sales conferences to sales representatives, the people who in turn sell the books to major bookstores and other outlets. She works with publicity and marketing staff, convincing them to spend time and money to promote her book, which is competing with other books in the house. She distributes advance copies to prominent people in the field (including other writers), hoping for favorable comments that can be used on the jacket or the cover. She is involved in planning the book's design, particularly its cover, which is a major sales tool. She will probably write copy for the jacket as well as for the publisher's sales catalog. (Publishers put out catalogs at regular intervals—usually two or three times a year—listing and describing all their new books and some backlist books as well; catalogs, too, are important sales tools.)

Along the way the editor holds the author's hand, keeping him informed about advertising and publicity strategies (e.g., print ads and TV interviews) and about each stage in the production process, letting him know when his manuscript will be returned to him to check the editing (and artwork, if any) and to answer editorial queries.

In addition to all these responsibilities, the senior editor somehow finds time to help shape the book itself.

"Shape" is the key word here. This editor is not primarily concerned with an author's turn of phrase or grammar. Her job is to evaluate the book as a whole and help the author make it the best it can be. This she does long before it goes into production—sometimes long before it is a book at all. (Most nonfiction books, because they require time-consuming and often costly research, are bought on the basis of a proposal and a couple of sample chapters. Some fiction is also bought this way, say a book from a well-known author, when even a few descriptive paragraphs might suffice, or a proposal for a romance novel that will conform to a specific formula.) She deals with structure and substance, style and pacing. She evaluates whether the book achieves its basic goal. In a book about a new kind of diet, the goal may be to explain why and how this particular approach works and why this diet is superior to the countless other diets on the market. In a mystery novel, the goal may be to entertain readers by sustaining the suspense and keep them guessing "who done it" until the novel's truly satisfying denouement.

As she reviews the manuscript, some of the questions the editor may ask herself are: Is the book a "good read"? Does its premise hold the reader's attention from beginning to end? If it is a novel, are the characters convincing and well developed? Is the story line plausible? Does the dialogue work?

If the answer to any of these questions is "no," the editor may suggest revisions, rewrites, or cuts. Her goal is to make the most salable book by helping the author express his or her ideas in the clearest and most effective way. At its best, the relationship between author and editor is a negotiating one, with give and take on both sides. The good editor suggests; she does not dictate. Compromises are worked out. The author may say, "I agree with you that the opening chapter is not strong enough. I will revise it. But the description of the rain forest in Chapter 4 must stay. I know it's long, but it helps create the foreboding atmosphere that sets the novel's tone." A smart editor will agree, perhaps saying to herself that it may be possible to shorten the rain forest scene at a later point in the editing process. Or, as the book develops, she may concur with the author's judgment.

Regrettably, in today's publishing climate, the shaping process we've just described is more the ideal than the norm. Considerations of time and money often intervene. For example, a mass-market editor who is handling four books a month and also looking for new ones won't have much time to devote to each individual project. The result is, only the most important (which generally translates into the most profitable) books are likely to get editorial loving care. Having stated that, we must qualify it by saying that the amount of editing done depends a lot on the individual editor's inclinations. One trade editor focuses her energies on acquiring a roster of high-powered authors and has little time left to work on the books themselves; a mass-market editor, on the other hand, cares so deeply about words that she feels compelled to line edit every book on her list.

The profile of the senior editor that follows is also the ideal. However, we've encountered a number of dedicated editors who come very close to achieving it.

Profile: The senior editor is first and foremost a voracious reader. She reads everything from newspapers to novels, and from encyclopedias and dictionaries to popular magazines. She is gregarious enough to get along with authors, illustrators, designers, and other editors, and to build good relationships with agents (an agent with whom she has a good working relationship is more likely to funnel worthwhile projects and good writers her way); she is aggressive enough to go after an author she admires and to "sell" a project she loves to her colleagues. She is a risk taker, creative enough to follow her instincts rather than slavishly follow trends. She is also an optimist: She believes in her books and authors and is ready to go to bat for them. She has to be flexible, because her day, if not her life, will involve a constant juggling of responsibilities. She is well organized and detail oriented, knowing how important it is to keep a "paper trail" for each project. She is practical as well as idealistic, never forgetting that publishing is a business and that books are products as well as creations of the imagination. And, like every editor worth her salt, she has a lifelong love affair with—and respect for—words.

Thomas McCormack, editorial director of St. Martin's Press, lists the following qualities of the ideal editor: "intelligence, sensitivity, tact, articulateness, industry, patience, accessibility, promptness, orderliness, thoroughness, a capacity to work alone, a capacity to work with others.

Plus sensibility and craft. No humans need apply."[1] To that we would add that good editors are made, not born, and almost always after long years of experience.

It should be noted that our description of the senior editor applies mainly to trade editors, that is, those involved with general fiction and nonfiction books. Editors in other areas of publishing—say, reference or textbooks—need many of the same skills, and some different ones as well. For more on these other areas of publishing, see Chapter 2, "Fact or Fiction? Finding Your Niche."

Line or Content Editor

The term "line editor" denotes a function rather than a title. Line or content editing—which involves substantive work on the manuscript—is sometimes done by the senior editor. More commonly, it is assigned to a lower-level staffer or else sent out to a freelancer. In these cases it will often be combined with copyediting.

Distinguishing between different types of editing isn't easy because no firm boundaries separate them. It helps to think of editing as a series of steps that go from the general to the specific. At one end is the senior editor, who deals with the big picture and often makes radical and sweeping suggestions. After reading the manuscript of a book on the automobile industry, she might ask the author to write a whole new chapter on the use of robots; she might suggest to the author of a first novel that a character change sex (e.g., become the protagonist's brother rather than his sister), believing that this would make the sibling relationship more powerful and also strengthen the plot. At the other end is the copyeditor, who will be looking through her microscope for a missing quotation mark or for a misnumbered footnote. (Which doesn't mean that a senior editor won't occasionally change a singular to a plural or that a copyeditor won't point out a plot flaw that slipped by the senior editor.)

[1] Thomas McCormack, *The Fiction Editor*. New York: St. Martin's Press, 1988, p. 71.

Line-editing functions lie somewhere between these two extremes. A priority for the line editor is to preserve an author's style. "Style" has two meanings for an editor. Here it connotes literary style, the way the writer writes. Style may also refer to house style—the publisher's or department's rules regarding spelling, capitalization, punctuation, and so on. Ensuring that house style is followed is the province of the copyeditor (see the section "Copyeditor," which follows).

The line editor asks himself certain questions as he reviews the manuscript. Has the author made herself clear? Do the characters sound like real people when they talk? Does the tone remain consistent throughout? (If, for example, she has chosen a formal style, a sudden change to slangy language would be jarring—and should be queried.) Has the author explained too much? (Beginning writers tend to overexplain because they haven't yet learned to trust their audience. Even experienced writers are often repetitious.) If the book is nonfiction, do the ideas follow one another logically? Are the terms well defined? Are the transitions clear?

When in doubt, the line editor queries the author, drawing attention to unclear passages, awkward phrasing, or missing or inaccurate information. He has more potential to intervene than the copyeditor and may revise or transpose copy to enhance the flow or strengthen the logic. But he will rewrite as little as possible and, when he does so, will make every effort to preserve the author's style. The line editor, like every other editor, must always keep in mind that the book is the author's, not his.

The preceding description—and it is by no means exhaustive—makes the line editor's job sound little short of overwhelming. Remember, though, that in practice he will not be called on to do all these things on every project. A well-written, carefully researched historical novel may require very little editing and may indeed be better off left mostly alone. On the other hand, an encyclopedia article on boats will require careful checking of every fact and the addition of any important aspect of the subject that hasn't been covered. If, for example, there is no mention of rafts, the editor might decide that they should be included. He will do some research on rafts and add a short paragraph. He may then need to tighten the article so it will fit into the allotted space; he will also check it for style and make it conform to the overall style established for the entire encyclopedia.

Profile: The line editor needs, above all, a special sensitivity to the written word. He empathizes with both what the writer is trying to achieve and the way the writer is trying to achieve it—his or her literary style. He avoids literal-mindedness and lets the writer write. He submerges his own ego to the writer's, not imposing his style or his way of thinking on the writer's work. He has a good ear for language, so that he can make the necessary changes without departing from the author's style and intent. And, like any good editor, he has a thorough command of grammar, spelling, and usage.

Copyeditor

The copyeditor is the workhorse of the editorial team. She must read the manuscript line for line, word for word, even letter for letter, looking for mistakes in grammar, usage, and spelling, for poor syntax, mixed metaphors, and non sequiturs. She also makes sure that house style, if any, is carefully adhered to.[2]

She changes sexist language, as well as wording that may be perceived as prejudiced in other ways (racist, ageist, ethnocentric), watches for the overuse of jargon or slang, for defamatory or potentially libelous statements, and for plagiarism. The copyeditor checks or queries any statement that seems inaccurate, whether in fiction or nonfiction, and often tracks down missing facts (Where was film director

[2] For sample style sheets, see Chapter 4, Figures 4.1 and 4.2.

Bernardo Bertolucci born? Who pitched the final baseball game for Cincinnati in the 1975 World Series? What was the estimated world catch of fish in 1987?) even if it means leafing through several reference books or making half a dozen phone calls. It helps if she has a good memory (was "healthcare" spelled as one word or two when it came up in Chapter 2?); it's essential that she have a questioning, even a suspicious mind.

In addition, the copyeditor receives instructions from the acquiring editor about what to look for in the manuscript and is alerted to special problems (e.g., overuse of italics for emphasis) or departures from conventional style (e.g., British spelling to be used instead of American). Dealing with these issues then becomes her responsibility.

The copyeditor also functions as a first proofreader. She reads to catch minutiae such as unclosed quotation marks, missing parentheses, or the wrong number of ellipsis points (periods . . . to show that something has been omitted). She checks that footnotes are styled consistently and numbered sequentially and that the table numbers in the text match the ones in the tables. She looks for transposed numerals (say, 1938 when 1983 is intended), makes sure percentages add up to one hundred, and alerts the author when the color of a character's sweater—or the shade of her lipstick—changes in the same scene.

In some houses, she is responsible for marking the manuscript for the typesetter (known as coding or typemarking). She uses special codes to show how elements such as chapter titles, subheads, and table titles will appear in print. She also instructs the typesetter on how tables, lists, extracts (long quotations), footnotes, and bibliographies are to be styled, marks words that are to be set in special type (e.g., **bold,** *italic,* or SMALL CAPS) and indicates when a new paragraph or a new page is required.

Part of the copyeditor's mandate is to sweat the small stuff. One copyeditor described this aspect of her job as follows: "It's a little like being what they used to call the continuity man or the script girl on a movie set—the person who makes sure the sun always rises in the same place and a glass of wine on a table is filled to the same level in every take. You have to get the details right in order for the big picture to emerge."

But because the copyeditor is frequently the only person to do extensive work on the manuscript, she may well find herself sweating the big stuff as well. Acquiring editors, pressed by the demands of the schedule and with a large list of books to handle, may have only enough time to skim through a manuscript. As a result, it's not unusual for a copyeditor to be asked to do substantive editing and copyediting at the same time.

Copyeditors are often blamed for the perceived decline of editing, but the real culprit is the limited time and resources available—the pressure of the bottom line.

Profile: In the words of one professional, "A copyeditor must be suited to the habit of sitting there looking earnestly at the shapes of words." To do so she has to have a good eye, which means being able to see textual mistakes and inconsistencies. (She may not be sure of the right spelling, but she can see that what's on the page is wrong.) She needs, in addition to a thorough knowledge of grammar and usage, a broad education and a familiarity with everything from ancient history to American neologisms. And she must, like every editor, be an avid reader.

Add to these traits a passion for accuracy, an avid curiosity, enormous patience, a zeal for detection—and meticulous attention to detail.

Attention to detail is what separates copyeditors from other editors. A good copyeditor is endlessly fussy, a nitpicker who will always take the time to look up a point of style for the umpteenth time until she is absolutely sure she has got it fixed in her head.

She is also comfortable working alone at her desk; she does not need constant interaction with other people. And she knows how to use tact and judgment in querying the author or other editors. Finally, she is not afraid to make decisions, aware that the editorial buck stops with her.

Proofreader

Though not considered editors, in practice proofreaders are another pair of editorial eyes. In fact, part of their job is to "pick up after" the copyeditor, finding errors of consistency, style, grammar, and so on that may have been overlooked.

Among the proofreader's many functions is to check for typographical errors ("typos") after the manuscript has been typeset. This he does by reading galleys (preliminary typeset pages) or pages (final pages with illustrations, tables, footnotes, etc., in place) against the copyedited manuscript.

Common typos include misspelled words, unclosed quotes, words repeated ("the the"), a capital letter where a lowercase one is needed ("Summer" instead of "summer"), a word set in italic (*savoir faire*) instead of roman type (savoir faire), and text set in the wrong font (typeface) or in the wrong type size.

The proofreader must be able to distinguish between an em dash—used to set off interjectional clauses—an en dash (used between a range of numbers, e.g., May 8–10, pp. 100–09), and a hyphen (used in combinations such as "self-respect" and "neo-Freudian"). He also checks the hyphens at the end of a line of type to be sure the words are broken in the right place (*fa-mous*, not *fam-ous*).

The proofreader also reads words, sentences, and paragraphs as a copyeditor does: for correctness, consistency, and sense. If he has been given a style sheet provided by the copyeditor, he will check that the style points have been followed—for example, "spell out numbers under 10; healthcare (n. and adj.) *but* health food (n. and adj.)." If he is reading page proofs, he also checks the layout; this means among other things seeing that any illustrations or tables appear on or close to the page where they are discussed, that heads—including running heads—are correctly placed, and that there is the prescribed amount of space above or below them.

The proofreader places corrections in the margin, not between the lines, so the typesetter will easily find the changes. He also marks each change to show whether it is a printer's error (PE) or an editor's alteration (EA). This is done because the typesetter is responsible for the cost of correcting PEs, but the publisher pays for EAs, as well as for AAs (author's alterations), at least up to a point.

Profile: A good proofreader has many of the traits of a good copyeditor—which he often aspires to be. (As we point out in Chapter 6, working as a proofreader can be an excellent stepping stone to an editing job. It is certainly the best training for such a job.) Ideally, a proofreader also has exceptionally sharp eyes; because he frequently has to deal with small print, he must be able to spot tiny differences in type sizes and unequal spacing between lines, words, or letters. (Proofreaders use a special ruler, called a pica ruler, to measure spacing.) The good proofreader reads slowly, not skipping over letters or words as a normal reader does, but carefully scrutinizing them. He isn't lulled into thinking that something is correct because it's in print, on a neat, clean, and final-looking page.

He also uses his judgment in making changes. Keeping in mind the high cost of making corrections once the type is set, he corrects glaring errors but lets go minor inconsistencies that do not affect sense. He also limits his queries to what is absolutely essential. At this stage, no editor will appreciate getting a set of pages covered with query flags that contain nitpicking comments about minor points of style.

As we've seen, editors of every kind have many functions in common. What subtly differentiates one from another was vividly summed up by an editor in chief at a trade publishing house: "When a senior editor reviews a manuscript, she is concerned with the big picture—she has to be able to see the forest for the trees. Line editors are also looking at the big picture, but they're just as interested in the elements that make up the picture, that give it color, shape, substance, and texture. They have to see the forest *and* the trees. Copyeditors, as well as proofreaders, are primarily concerned with the details that make the picture accurate, coherent, and pleasing to the eye. Their job is to painstakingly examine every leaf on every tree in the forest." (For a summary of the stages of editing, see the accompanying list.)

STAGES OF EDITING

Type of editing	Done by
Editorial review (for structure, plot, completeness, tone, pace, characterization, etc.)	Acquiring editor
Line editing (for content, author's style, clarity, flow, etc.)	Acquiring editor, copyeditor, or junior staff member
Copyediting (for house style, grammar, usage, sexism, accuracy, etc.)	Copyeditor (in-house or freelance)
Proofreading (for typesetting errors, house style, page layout, etc.)	Proofreader (in-house or freelance)

Some editors, despite their titles, do little or no editing. One example is the *production editor*. In simple terms, his job is to oversee the progress of a manuscript through every phase of production from manuscript to bound book. He may set schedules or just ensure that as far as possible each phase is completed on time. The production editor ferries material between copyeditors, designers, illustrators, and proofreaders (in-house staff or freelancers), then sends it back to the acquiring editor and the author; he transmits the final manuscript to the compositor (typesetter), sometimes as "hard copy" (a computer printout or typewritten manuscript), sometimes on disks, sometimes over a modem, which transfers it directly from the publisher's computer into the typesetter's. When the copy comes back to him in the form of galley or page proofs, he gets these checked and corrected, then circulates them again to whoever needs to see them. The finished product, in the form of film or camera copy (high-quality proof that is photographed to make film) is sent to the printer. The end product is, of course, a bound book. The production editor may also be responsible for keeping track of costs, getting estimates from suppliers such as the typesetter and the printer, checking bills, and authorizing payments. His duties can vary from house to house even though the title remains the same.

The *managing editor* is usually an administrator or department head who supervises other editors, including production editors, and may draw up budgets and set salaries. She may also "manage" the schedule, in which case her duties are similar to the production editor's.

Theme and Variations

Having defined some variations of the editorial species, we hasten to add that the categories are more theoretical than actual. In real life, editing functions almost always overlap, largely for reasons of economy. A big publishing house or division may be able to afford the luxury of breaking down editing tasks and assigning them to specialized staff members. A smaller one is more likely to ask the same editor to handle more than one function; a copyeditor may also be the proofreader; a production editor may copyedit the manuscript as well as supervise its production. Often, little or no editing of any kind is done in-house; the manuscript is instead farmed out to a freelance editor. More and more, publishing houses are cutting costs by using the services of freelance editors and proofreaders, which allows them to operate with a smaller full-time staff.

Classifying editors is also complicated by the fact that editors with the same or similar titles are apt to have different responsibilities at different publishing houses.

At the top of the pyramid, just below the publisher or the head of the house, is the *editor in chief,* or *editorial director.* The editor in chief runs an editorial department, which may be a large group or just a handful of people. He has overall responsibility for the list (all the books acquired), sets the direction for the type of books he wants to publish, and is involved in the choice of individual books. He develops strategies to ensure the success of his list and sets priorities for sales and promotion; he guides his senior editors and keeps in close touch with sales, publicity, and rights staff. He is responsible for the staffing of the department and for drawing up its budget. And all the while, he must worry about where his next list is coming from.

As an administrator, he must also deal with personnel problems—those which arise between editors or other staff, those which involve difficult authors and agents. Sometimes the problems are on a more mundane level. The editor in chief of a dictionary told of hearing loud screams coming from down the hall one day, which brought him running out of his office. The cause was a huge water bug, which had been sighted in the library, terrifying most of the staff. "I found it sitting on a large tome," he said, "appropriately enough, a book about insects. Since no one else was willing to touch it, it fell to me to kill the bug. It's all part of a day's work."

Some editors in chief have their own lists and their own stable of authors, and some even find time to edit the books on their list. It depends on the individual and also on the size of the publisher or the division. An editorial director in charge of a five-person children's book division carefully shepherds her books through editing and production. The head of a major encyclopedia with a staff of around twenty is involved in the selection of every new article and reviews every article before it goes to print. On the other hand, the editor in chief of a mass-market division that publishes around 300 books a year devotes most of her time to sales and marketing, traveling extensively to sales conferences and book fairs. While she has the final say on what's published, she does little acquiring and has no hands-on contact with the books themselves.

Some acquiring editors are hired solely to sign up books and develop them from a marketing point of view. This is particularly true in textbook publishing, where the acquiring editors aren't necessarily literary types (though they must have a college degree). College editors are generally drawn from the sales staff and are more involved in the business of publishing than in the business of words. In the case of textbooks, another editor (sometimes called a project editor or an editing supervisor) takes over once the author delivers a finished manuscript. (See the section "College Textbooks" in Chapter 2.)

Encyclopedia and yearbook editors acquire articles rather than books, and acquiring is only a small part of their jobs, which involve heavy research and much rewriting. Editors at other types of reference houses may not acquire at all; this is true in dictionary departments, where almost all the writing is done by in-house staff, although consultants with expertise in special fields will be called in to review some of the material. (See Chapter 2 for more on reference editors.)

At the entry level are *editorial assistants*, who are generally considered to be editors in training. (In a few areas, however, notably textbook publishing, the job is essentially secretarial and not on the editing track.) Next on the ladder are *assistant* and *associate editors*, who will almost certainly do some editing, although the extent will vary with the house.

The editorial assistant spends her day performing a multitude of mundane tasks, which may include logging in manuscripts as they arrive, typing letters to authors and agents, filling out endless numbers and varieties of forms, writing away for permissions to reprint material, sending faxes, making photocopies (sometimes of entire manuscripts), answering phones, and filing, filing, filing. But the position of editorial assistant is truly what you decide to make it. (For more on this, see the section "Getting Ahead" in Chapter 2.)

As we made our way through an editorial department, we pointed out how many editing jobs overlap. We should add that, because publishing is not a highly stratified field, editors at almost any level are likely to spend a fair amount of time on routine tasks: obtaining permissions, sending form rejection letters to authors or agents, even standing at the photocopying machine. And most of them answer their own phones, assistants being in short supply except at the highest levels. (This means that when you're job hunting, you have a good chance of reaching by phone any editor you're interested in working for.) In short, today's editor is expected to be a jack of all trades. To get ahead, she must be a master of them as well.

Editing by the Book

Editors can also be classified in a different way—by the type of books they edit. Most people associate editors with trade books—books that can be found in general bookstores and that take up most of the space on bestseller lists.

Trade books, which include fiction and nonfiction as well as some popular reference books such as "how-to's," are intended for a general readership. They are published by trade book houses (or divisions), among which you will find publishing's most familiar—and distinguished—names. Trade book editors generally handle both fiction and non-fiction, although some specialize in one or the other.

Most of the "quality" (nonformulaic) fiction being published today can be labeled "mainstream." ("Experimental" novels are deemed financially risky by many houses and are usually published by small presses, or sometimes by university presses.) Collections of short stories and of poetry (which are usually previously published before a collection is considered) also fall into this category.

Nonfiction is a very broad category; it includes biography, history, and politics, art and culture, travel and leisure, as well as collections of essays—in most cases also previously published—ranging from the personal to the philosophical.

A subdivision of fiction is mass market. This category comprises the inexpensive paperbacks that are sold in airports, supermarkets, drugstores, stationery stores, and other retail outlets. Mass-market books include genre fiction—romances, sci-fi, westerns, Gothic novels, and mysteries, to name a few—and some commercial nonfiction, such as self-help books, sports books, and New Age (which encompasses everything from mysticism to meditation and massage). Most trade books are first published in hardcover editions; trade, or quality paperbacks (as distinguished from mass market), usually published by the same house, will follow if the book is successful. In recent years, there has been a growing trend toward publishing paperback originals. These are less expensive than hardcovers both to produce and to buy, making them accessible to a wider public.

As with almost everything in publishing, there is considerable overlap between trade and mass market. More and more large publishers have set up their own paperback divisions, which reprint their successful trade books in mass-market editions. And some mass-market divisions even publish a few original hardcover books of their own.

Children's books, both fiction and nonfiction, have their own departments and their own editors. Most are published as trade books, but mass-market children's books—many of which are books older children can afford to buy for themselves—also constitute an important area. Children's books are divided by age groups, ranging from picture books and

board books for the youngest "readers" to books for beginning readers, middle readers, and teenagers (the last category is known as young adult or YA books). Some editors
of juvenile books choose to specialize—for example, in picture books, which are heavily dependent on illustrations—
while others handle books for all age groups.

Other segments of the book market are college textbooks,
elementary and high school books (known as "el-hi"), professional books (e.g., advanced books on medicine, the sciences, or philosophy—many of which are published by university presses), religious books, including Bibles, and
reference books (encyclopedias, almanacs, dictionaries, some
how-to's, and many others that provide and classify information). Each type of book—and our list is not exhaustive—
has its own special demands and requires its own set of
editorial skills.

Chapter 2 explores the various segments of the book market and offers career advice to the editor-to-be.

The Winding Road from Manuscript
to Bound Book

The road from manuscript to bound book—a journey taken
by every book in the making—is never a smooth or straight
one. The manuscript moves from editor to editor, with each
one along the route sending messages to colleagues—either
those who have preceded her or those who will follow. The
journey will include side trips—to the designer, the illus-
trator, or the production department, and back to the author (generally more than once) to get his answers to editors'
queries, to have him approve illustrations or biographical
material to go on the jacket.

This backing and forthing complicates the editorial process and contributes to the blurring of functions. It is also
its greatest strength, because it provides checks and balances
that help polish the book and cut down the number of po-

tential errors. Editors check other editors, production people check design, proofreaders check everyone else—and authors have a chance to make sure the book they are getting is the book they set out to write.

The journey begins with the senior editor. By the time she receives the final version of the manuscript, the editor will (ideally, at least) have worked out any major problems with the author, probably through submitting a list of broad, general queries. In her editorial letter, she may have suggested organizational changes, rewrites, or cuts (e.g., "pp. 68ff.: This paragraph is substantially the same as para. 3, p. 56. Possible to delete?"). If editing fiction, she probably pointed out structural weaknesses (e.g., "This is an intricate mystery that you've built slowly and meticulously. Its abrupt ending might leave readers dissatisfied. Any thoughts?") as well as "soft spots" in plot and characterization ("Chap. 4: Dewey has been best friends with Frank for years; would he really cut him off so abruptly? Possible to supply additional motivation?").

The senior editor's task now is to "stage manage" the book's production, checking the "script" and the "stage directions," answering questions, monitoring everyone else's performance, and making final decisions. She also continues as the author's advocate, letting him know what to expect—and what's expected of him—at every stage.

Once she has read the manuscript, she will alert the copyeditor to particular problems she foresees, either on flags she attaches to individual pages or by means of a query sheet, which will include page and line numbers for easy reference.

"Watch out for inconsistencies in spelling of foreign names—see pp. 10, 43, and 219," her note might read. Or: "Too many 'ain't's' in the dialogue in Chap. 4, pp. 63–64. Reword some of them or cut." She may also alert the copyeditor to exceptions to house style that she—or the author—prefers. ("Follow author's style on bibliography. Check for consistency only." Or, "Note my preference for President, not president, of U.S.")

If an author has a tendency to be redundant—to overuse a word or phrase or repeat the same point—the acquiring editor may instruct the copyeditor to flag instances for the author's attention; or she may instruct him to vary or delete them at his own discretion.

The copyeditor will have messages of his own to send back up the line to his boss. He may suggest substantive changes he does not have the authority to make himself. He will alert her to any "surprises" he comes across in the manuscript, for example, a derogatory reference to a real person that he recognizes as potentially libelous, or the description of a specific incident that sounds suspiciously like something he has read elsewhere (and may be a case of plagiarism).

The copyeditor also carries on a dialogue with the author via the flags he attaches to the manuscript pages, querying points of substance and style (e.g., "Betty describes her uncle's attempt to seduce her in almost the same language on pp. 24 and 75. Possible to vary one?" "Note use of passive voice in three successive sentences. OK to fix as I've indicated?") (Query etiquette is discussed in the section "Tact" in Chapter 3.)

The author becomes an active player when he receives the edited manuscript. It is the author's responsibility to assiduously study—and either approve or disapprove—all editorial suggestions or changes. Some authors balk at changes, but most recognize—and are grateful for—editing that makes a better book.

After the manuscript is returned, the copyeditor (or in some cases the production editor) carefully incorporates the author's responses into it. (This invariably means overturning earlier decisions—a strong argument for always editing in erasable colored pencil, not pen!)

The last link in the editorial chain is the proofreader, who will read the book in pages and often checks final corrections. She may also find herself, flags in hand, querying mistakes and lapses in consistency missed by the copyeditor.

It is a rare proofreader who will not pick up errors that have slipped by all who have previously seen the manuscript.

At the final stage, the proofreader is all that stands between editors and authors and their worst nightmares, chief among which are dropped pages, transposed paragraphs, and lines set twice. (We've heard many horror stories: In one book, the table of contents was omitted from the printed book; in another, half of the final chapter was left out.)

It takes an average of nine to twelve months after the submission of the final manuscript for a book to be published. Our focus in this book is on editing and the editorial phase of a book's life. For those interested in production and design and how they mesh with the editing process, we recommend Marshall Lee's standard work *Bookmaking: The Illustrated Guide to Design, Production, Editing*, 2nd ed. New York: R. R. Bowker, 1979.

Chapter 2

Fact or Fiction?
Finding Your Niche

Let us suppose you're a recent college graduate whose heart
is set on a career in editing. Or, you've worked for a couple
of years in the publicity department of a publishing house
and are interested in switching to the editorial side. Or else
you're a production editor who's just completed a copyediting course and would like a job that involves more editing. Over the course of several weeks, you've scanned the
"Help Wanted" section of your newspaper and found three
ads that intrigued you (see ads on next page).

You'll note that all three jobs advertised involve a great
deal of routine office work. Ad A, a position with a prestigious university press, specifies "administrative support
service, organizational abilities," "accurate typing skills,"
and "computer/word processing experience." Ad B wants
an "energetic, detail-oriented candidate" who will assist two
editors at a children's book house with "phones, correspondence, filing." Ad C, which describes a job with a mass-
market publisher, requires "general office duties" as well as
some copyediting expertise and computer skills.

You may also note that Ad A differs from the other two in
an important respect: *It does not mention any editing-related
work*, such as reading manuscripts or proofreading. This
doesn't mean that the Ad A job won't eventually give you a
chance to edit. It does mean that you should check this out
if you are interviewed for the job. If you want to be an editor, there's no point in taking a job that will not lead in that
direction.

EDITORIAL ASSISTANT
SCIENCE/MEDICINE

We are a respected publishing firm currently seeking an Editorial Assistant capable
of providing a full range of administrative
support service to the Executive Editor,
Medicine and Science. The individual we
seek must possess excellent organizational
abilities, accurate typing skills, a pleasant
phone manner & the ability to communicate on a professional level. Com-
puter/word processing experience is required. Please send resumé to:

Ad A

EDITORIAL ASSISTANT

Upscale children's book publisher seeks
energetic, detail-oriented candidate for
editorial assistant position. Responsibilities
include assisting two editors with phones,
correspondence, filing, as well as reading
manuscripts and writing copy. Forward
resumé and salary history to:

Ad B

ASSISTANT EDITOR

Well-known mass market publisher seeks
ass't editor for manuscript reading and
evaluation, copyediting, and general office
duties. Knowledge of mystery fiction a +.
Knowledge of WordPerfect pref. Reply in
writing only, with salary req., to:

Ad C

Knowing how hard it is to get that first editing job, the three of you may take a chance and answer all these ads. What you may not realize as you send off your resumé is that the job you choose (or, more likely, the job that chooses you) may affect the whole course of your editing career.

You may wonder why this is so, arguing that editing is editing. You'd be right, at least in theory. The same basic skills—a command of grammar, usage, and style, an eye for detail, a feel for language, a love of words—come into play, whether you are editing a scholarly work on psychology, a children's book, or a detective novel (although, as we shall see in this chapter, each subject area does have its own special demands). The problem is, while skills are transferable, transferring yourself is another matter.

Publishing tends to pigeonhole people quite early in their careers. Trade departments like to hire people with trade experience (at least for higher-level jobs); reference departments quite naturally give priority to applicants with reference experience. A senior editor with a textbook department would have a hard time getting a comparable job in trade; a mass-market editor who'd been editing mysteries for five years and who decided what he really wanted was to work in children's books would find it difficult to make the switch. Part of the problem is that a senior editor must know the market—who's publishing what, who are the best writers in the field, which agents specialize in what books, and so on—and that kind of knowledge is acquired only by years of experience.

Which is not to say that switching fields is impossible. We've heard of an encyclopedia editor who went on to make a fine career with a trade publisher; we know another editor who, after knocking on many doors, found a job with a trade publisher after having worked on teenage romances. ("Going from genre to trade," she said, "is always a hard move. It's even worse if you're going from children's books to adult because people don't think children's books are real books. The same goes for business books. It's largely a question of snobbery.") We've also come across one or two editors who were willing to start over—which meant taking a job at or close to the bottom and a salary cut—in order to work in the subject area of their choice.

But switching is never easy. Which is why we recommend that, before embarking on a career in editing, you find out as much as you can about the different subject areas. And that if you aren't happy in the field that you've started in, you consider a change early in your career.

The overall editing process has been described in detail in Chapter 1. In this chapter we'll give you a sense of the differences between major areas—in terms of the environment as well as the work itself—and help you decide where you'll best fit in.

A Novel Approach: Editing Fiction

Quality Fiction

To most outsiders, editing fiction is the glamorous part of publishing. Other kinds of editing just don't measure up.

The reality, though, is that novels—or, at any rate, literary novels—form a very small part of the book market today. People are more likely to read nonfiction or genre fiction (which includes romances, mysteries, sci-fi, occult, and Westerns as well as many of the blockbusters that appear on bestseller lists). For prospective editors, this means their chance to edit a great novel is quite small—and that they should at least consider other areas of publishing.

"When I went on my first interviews," a fiction editor related, "I was forewarned by some kindly elder publishing type never to say I wanted to go into publishing because I was interested in literature. I promptly disobeyed. A love of good books won't really help you develop your career, but for me, at least, it makes the business of publishing bearable."

On the whole, the publishing industry takes a jaundiced view of so-called literary, or quality, fiction—and with good reason. Novels and collections of short stories and poetry usually don't sell, and they often end up losing money for a publisher. This doesn't mean that "Literature" (with a capital "L") won't continue to be published, for prestige if for nothing else. But as fiction sales in general continue to decline (approximately 4,800 works of fiction were published in 1993, roughly the same number as in the previous year, and comprising only about 11 percent of all trade books published[1]), literary editors, like prestigious old-line publishing houses, have had to diversify and acquire more commercial properties, both fiction and nonfiction, in order to survive.

Quality fiction doesn't sell, according to conventional wisdom, because most people want to be entertained, not challenged. This unfortunate split between what is perceived as art and entertainment is relatively recent. From Sophocles to Shakespeare and down to Charles Dickens and Mark Twain in the nineteenth century, works regarded as literature were also popular reading, managing to entertain as well as edify. But by the twentieth century, two separate novelistic strains, which were before interwoven, began to emerge—the novel as adventure and escape, and the novel as personal exploration and psychological revelation. One genre editor who specializes in romance put it succinctly: "Genre is in the tradition of epic storytelling; the 'modern' novel has existential, even Freudian roots."

Another possible reason for today's readers' disaffection with quality fiction, which, according to John Gardner, has at its center "character," is that it is too slow for our modern world of action movies and MTV. According to Gardner, "The writer's business is to make up convincing human beings and create for them basic situations and actions by which they come to know themselves and reveal themselves to the reader."[2] Building characters is a slow, incremental process. Commercial fiction, by contrast, tends to be plot-driven, fast, a good read. Interestingly, those genre writers

[1] Source: "Inching Ahead," *Publishers Weekly*, March 7, 1994, p. S32.
[2] John Gardner, *The Art of Fiction*. New York: Random House, 1991, p. 15.

who transcend their form—for instance, P. D. James in mystery and John le Carré in intrigue—are usually writers who develop a character through a series of books or, like Ursula Le Guin and Ray Bradbury in sci-fi, treat as their subject what has always been the primary subject of serious fiction—"human emotion, values, and beliefs."[3]

For those who choose to "disobey" economic imperatives and become literary editors, taste, sensitivity, and tact, along with a basic understanding of human psychology, are essential.

Literary editors need to know psychology because they have to do a lot of persuading and negotiating, with agents and authors as well as with their colleagues (to sell fiction in-house, which is often the hardest sell). Fiction editors buy most of their books from literary agents. (Unsolicited manuscripts, if they are read at all, are first screened by an editorial assistant who will only rarely recommend one to a senior editor.) They must therefore work hard to establish good relationships with agents who know their taste, and whose taste they trust. One editor, who defines literary writing as "style-oriented," looks for "writerly fiction," and the agents she deals with know exactly what she wants.

Agents are also important because they function as the gatekeepers to the publishing world. They receive almost as many unsolicited submissions as editors do; if a good agent takes on someone new, especially a literary writer, chances are that writer's work is at least worth a look by an editor. The busiest editor will usually read a manuscript submitted by a trusted agent and take the time to respond personally, even if it's with a rejection.

Another reason for an editor to cultivate good relationships with agents is that agents can facilitate an editor's personal dealings with writers. In today's volatile publishing market, where editors come and go, agents are increasingly taking over the editor's traditional role as a writer's anchor and confidant. The one constant in a shifting world, an agent frequently exerts considerable editorial influence over a writer's work.

[3] Ibid., p. 14.

"Negotiating" with authors in the context of the author/editor relationship is covered in Chapter 5, "The Editor's Sensibility." Suffice it to say here that if you want to line edit manuscripts as well as acquire them, quality fiction may be for you. One editor described line editing as the "privilege of the impoverished" because "no one's going to do it if I don't. And why handle these kinds of books if you're not going to give them this kind of attention?" In other words, she sees line editing not as a chore but as one of the rewards of her job.

There are also solid practical reasons for literary editors to do line editing. One editor pointed out that if you don't line edit a book, you really don't have a feel for it, you don't share the author's passion. In his view, that lack of passion will ultimately be detrimental to publicity and sales. On the other hand, when you get to know and love a book through line editing it, "others in-house will feel what you felt and respond to your enthusiasm."

Not surprisingly, each editor has an individual approach to fiction editing. One editor told us she rarely takes on a book that isn't well crafted; she tries to stay away from manuscripts that appear to have real problems of style and syntax. "If I find myself working very, very hard trying to improve the style of a fiction writer, I come away from the book feeling disappointed, no matter what the outcome." But another editor delighted in relating how he had guided a promising but still raw young writer and helped him discover his own style.

For the editor of literary fiction, the rewards range from discovering an exciting new author to nurturing another until his "breakthrough" book comes along to helping a third find her own voice. One editor, who described herself as a "reality check" for writers, spends a lot of energy reminding her writers that it's a hard road from beginning to end and that, no matter how worthy they are, when it comes to literary fiction, nothing can be taken for granted—not good reviews or good sales and, least of all, success. "I just hope that they will derive pleasure from what I think is most important—perfecting their work. And not getting side-tracked or confused or devastated by the reception of the outside world."

What Makes a Good Quality Fiction Editor?
- The ability to care and feel passionate about good writing.
- A literary sensibility.
- The ability to be an attentive reader and a good listener.
- Gregariousness coupled with good interpersonal skills.
- An understanding of human nature.
- A compassionate heart combined with an objective eye.

Mass-market Fiction

"A lot of people don't think they read genre books, but they do. They read mysteries or thrillers or historical novels, for example, but they don't think of them as genre, because they look down on genre."

The comment came from a senior editor at a mass-market publisher whose specialty is historical romances. The facts back her up—most fiction bought today is in the form of mass-market paperbacks, books selected for their appeal to the widest possible audience and printed in large quantities, often more than 100,000 copies. These are the books you'll find in supermarkets, airports, drugstores, and convenience stores, as well as in bookstores, in particular the large chains.

Mass-market publishers are often part of larger publishing houses. Many hardcover publishers have set up their own paperback divisions, which allows them to publish the paperback editions of their own bestselling books.

Editing mass-market books is similar to editing general trade books. What distinguishes mass market is the quantity of books produced. A general trade editor may be responsible for as many as fifteen to twenty books a year; a mass-market editor may handle four books a month—close to fifty a year. Some of these are reprints that require little if any editing, but that is still a heavy editorial load.

The career mass-market editor is very often a devoted fan of the genre he or she edits, and such people make the best editors. Says one romance editor: "A lot of women share the fantasy and have read this kind of stuff for years. One woman, who was a lawyer, loved this kind of book and wanted to edit them. She contacted heads of romance book departments at a whole bunch of publishers and nagged them until she ended up getting a job, and a pretty good one at that."

Market savvy is crucial in this field, much more so than doing hands-on work on the manuscript. Acquiring editors must buy well and sell well; and they must have the confidence to go to auction and commit (or decide not to commit) large sums of their publisher's money. Like other editors, they work closely with sales and promotion people, write copy for the sales catalog, and supervise the art and design for the covers. What goes on the cover is crucial (particularly when the author is an unknown). Because paperbacks are rarely reviewed, the covers are a major sales tool, and a lot of time—and often a lot of money—is spent on them. Eye-catching covers with embossed titles and brightly colored foil are often what sells a book to the casual supermarket shopper or the airport traveler browsing at a carousel.

Most mass-market books fall into categories or genres, since a book that fulfills the demand of a special segment of the reading public is—in theory, at least—less of a gamble than a book that cannot be labeled. A category is a bit like a brand name, and, significantly, bookstores now arrange books in categories and label the shelves accordingly.

Most editors specialize in one genre or another: sci-fi, romance, mystery, horror, Westerns. There are also categories within categories: the romance category, which is huge, comprises historical and contemporary, time travel and romantic suspense, sweet and innocent romances and sexy and titillating ones; mysteries include traditional detective stories, legal thrillers, and women's mysteries, known as "cozies," because they have a woman sleuth and feature less blood and gore.

Each category has its own set of conventions, often narrowly defined. The murder mystery demands a solution, the romance novel a happy ending, sci-fi books use a common lingo treasured by their devoted fans. Some publishers supply would-be authors with guidelines known as tip sheets, which outline what they're looking for in a particular category or in a line within that category. In romance, although the requirements are less specific and less rigid than in the past, the hero and heroine must still fit certain molds. The hero in one line must be "bold, brash and brave," in another, "attractive, compelling, and powerful," in a third, "an unpredictable, rough-edged bad boy." Heroines often have to be "sassy," "spirited," or "spunky," as well as "emotionally vulnerable," but not necessarily virginal anymore. Explicit sex descriptions, once taboo, are permitted in some lines, but sex must always be tied to love. As one tip sheet puts it, "The emphasis should be on shared emotions as well as sensual feelings."

An exciting aspect of being an editor in this area of publishing is that the genres are by no means static. As we've just seen, romance conventions have evolved to reflect changing sexual and social mores. Moreover, new genres keep popping up in response to cultural trends; for example, in the late 1980s we had suspense novels on the theme of women in danger, followed by the woman-as-predator genre, as exemplified by the movie *Fatal Attraction*.

Sometimes—and this is the dream of a mass-market editor—a genre book will transcend a particular category and become the latest blockbuster bestseller. Knowing this can happen is part of what attracts people to this branch of publishing. Examples of writers who made this jump are Ann Rice (horror), Danielle Steele (romance), Michael Crichton (fantasy/sci-fi), John Grisham (legal thriller), and Sue Grafton (women's mystery).

A senior editor who handles women's fiction (from mainstream novels to romantic suspense) described the appeal of her job as follows: "It's very lively. It's fun. Your job is to read fun things that hopefully you'll enjoy. It's also extremely challenging. If a book you're interested in goes to auction and you bid on it, that's exciting. There's a certain amount of travel, you can go to conferences, speak on panels, lunch with literary agents, if you enjoy that. I also read a lot, and browse in bookstores. It's very fast-paced, frenetic even. Some people might not like that, but I love it."

What mass-market editing does not offer is prestige, at least within the industry. But to successful editors in the field, that's less important than being able to buy and edit books that they themselves enjoy reading.

What Makes a Good Mass-market Editor?
- A genuine liking for a particular genre.
- A knowledge of the market—what the audience for each genre expects.
- A taste for the fast pace and excitement of this brand of editing.
- The ability to work under pressure.
- A gregarious disposition.

On-the-Job Learning: Editing Nonfiction

Merriam-Webster defines nonfiction as "literature that is not fictional." And, according to one nonfiction editor, "what is not fiction is less than fiction, or at least that's been the bias."

This "bias" is largely a holdover from the nineteenth century, which favored the so-called literary forms of the novel, short story, and poetry. But times, and the tastes and needs of the reading public, change. The twentieth century, especially since World War II, has seen nonfiction take its place as what William Zinsser describes as the "new American literature."[4]

The proof of this statement is in sales: The vast majority

[4] William Zinsser, *On Writing Well: An Informal Guide to Writing Nonfiction*, 4th ed. New York: HarperCollins, 1990, p. 56.

of trade books published today are nonfiction. The reasons for this are fairly straightforward. Nonfiction's reality orientation seems to suit the sensibility of modern readers. Instead of the opaqueness and revelation of literary fiction, nonfiction offers immediacy and information—and more than anything else, the book-buying public seems to want information, about their own lives as well as the world around them.

Contemporary nonfiction writers tackle a host of topics: biography and popular history and culture, contemporary politics and exposés (such as tell-all books about the Clinton White House, the scoop on the corporate raiders of the 1980s, or the latest celebrity biography offering revelations about a movie star's private life), books on sports and hobbies, travel and leisure books, cookbooks and computer books. And, of course, how-to's—on everything from how to improve your love life to how to get more miles to the gallon to how to edit fact and fiction. All these fall under the category of nonfiction.

Among the most distinguished (and popular) present-day writers who write primarily nonfiction are Tom Wolfe and Joan Didion (popular culture), John McPhee and Annie Dillard (nature and human nature), Roger Angell and Tom Boswell (baseball and the American experience), Oriana Fallaci (politics and oral history), and Anna Quindlen (personal essay). Well-known fiction writers have also contributed major nonfiction works, notably Truman Capote, Norman Mailer, and Gore Vidal. In his "roster of the new literature," Zinsser includes

> all the writers who come bearing information, who explain what they know clearly, and who make an arrangement of it that raises their craft to an art. In an age when survival is tenuous and events outrun our ability to make sense of them, these are important writers.[5]

Just as many writers work in both fiction and nonfiction,

[5] Ibid., p. 57.

editors usually edit both, although most specialize in one or the other. In the words of a predominantly fiction editor: "What's closest to me is working on books whose ideas engage me, and that's happened with me with nonfiction as well."

In acquiring nonfiction, the idea *is* the thing. As opposed to a novel, which usually has to be completed before being considered, nonfiction is most often bought on the basis of a proposal, an outline, and perhaps a sample chapter or two. One editor told us that when a proposal comes in, the first thing he looks for is credentials—is this author the best person to write this book? Essentially, "you look for someone who has the ability to get the book out there to its audience." Credentials are a powerful marketing tool for selling the book both to in-house colleagues and the reading public.

The proposal, also a sales tool, affords an editor a first look at an author's writing style. One editor said he can tell very quickly from a cover letter, or two or three pages of a proposal, whether the author is a professional and he wants to work with him or her for the two years or so it takes to make a book. But another editor observed that writers of good books can be lousy proposal writers and vice versa. "So you can get a wonderful proposal on a really crazy, confused manuscript. You never know what to expect—that's part of the fun, and part of the peril, of editing nonfiction."

Nonfiction editing, like fiction editing, demands that the editor respect the author's style and intent. But in nonfiction, the principal goal is to convey information to the reader. Because the editor works to clarify an author's words and strengthen the organization of his ideas, she has more leeway than the fiction editor.

Fact checking is particularly important in nonfiction editing. Although the author is ultimately responsible for the accuracy of the work, the editor must have an instinct about which facts should be verified—or queried—and must know where to go to check them. She must also have an eye open for potential legal problems (such as libel, plagiarism, and invasion of privacy) that might arise from statements in a text. To avoid such problems, one editor alerts authors from the start about the kind of documentation they need to keep, for example, tape-recorded interviews and sources for quotations. "If you prepare an author well," he said, "you'll avoid ending up with a book that has to be shredded."

Nonfiction editors can't be experts in every area in which they accept manuscripts. Nor should they be. The best nonfiction editors tend to be generalists with broad interests and a knowledge of many topics. As one editor remarked, "A side benefit of editing nonfiction is that you learn new things every day and deepen the knowledge you already have—and how many jobs can you say that about?"

Still, editors should know enough about a subject to ask the questions that a book's potential readership would ask. And part of the nonfiction editor's job is to know who the experts in certain fields are—and to call them in to evaluate the viability of a project or to vet a completed manuscript. The editor must also know how much weight should be given to reviewers' comments because he is the one who makes the decision whether or not to publish.

While nonfiction editors use agents to acquire manuscripts, they are less dependent on them than fiction editors are. Ideas for fiction (quality fiction, at any rate) are generated by the writer, and the editor can only wait for the creative process to run its course. In nonfiction, however, an editor doesn't have to wait for agents to plop things in his lap. He can pick up the phone and call a writer whose work he admires—perhaps he's seen an article he liked in *Harper's* magazine or a story in *People*—and suggest she write a book on a particular subject. Nonfiction can be a good place for an energetic newcomer to start because "it's easy for a twenty-four-year-old to sign up his or her first book that way," according to one senior editor.

One editor who predominantly edits nonfiction explained his love for his work this way: "In nonfiction, there's always the slim chance that you can do something of consequence, something that can make something better or influence someone. You have the capacity for change."

What Makes a Good Nonfiction Editor?
- The ability to care and feel passionate about ideas and writing.
- The ability to generate new ideas.
- A broad general knowledge of current events, issues, and people in the news.
- The drive to acquire projects aggressively.
- The ability to sell a book in-house and market it effectively.
- Gregariousness coupled with good interpersonal skills.

Getting the Picture: Editing Children's Books

What distinguishes children's books from other kinds can be summed up in a word: variety. Today there are books for children of every age, from babies of a few weeks old to teenagers close to graduation. The subject matter is equally varied; it includes fiction, fact and fancy, poetry and prose, jokes and riddles, biography and sports, nature and how-to.

Furthermore, the books come in an astonishing variety of shapes and sizes and materials—a far cry from the standard oblong clothbound or paperbound adult books. There are fabric books, plastic books, and board books, round books and square books, tiny books and huge books, books shaped like trains or boats or houses, books to go into the bathtub or to comfort a toddler in bed, pop-up books, lift-the-flap books that reveal the insides of a plane or train, kit books that let you make a stand-up panorama of a rain forest.

Today's children's books are more than words on paper: They are complex productions in which illustrations, text, and other elements are closely integrated.

Fortunately, perhaps, not all editors edit every kind of book. The books are broken down into age groups, beginning with the youngest readers and going in stages to books for children of twelve and up, known as young adult, or YA, books. The groupings are somewhat arbitrary and often overlap. Publishers' decisions on how to classify a book depend on factors such as age of the main character and the length of the book.

Some editors specialize in particular age groups or subject areas—picture books for the youngest children, teenage fiction, nonfiction books about science or nature, "problem" books treating subjects such as divorce, drugs, or stepfamilies—while others, particularly in small houses or departments, handle a wide range.

Children's book editors acquire in much the same way as other editors, except that they must know how to buy illustrations as well as text. While some books come in with both text and illustrations, in general the editor buys a manuscript and finds an artist to illustrate it. Buying art for children's books *is* an art. The editor must have the sensitivity to know the kind of illustrations that will enhance and illuminate the text, to match the artist to the writer.

A children's book editor must also know how to edit art. Editing art means reviewing it (1) for internal consistency and (2) to make sure the pictures match the text.

Checking for this particular form of consistency is a little like making sure that words are spelled or hyphenated the same way throughout a manuscript. For example, in one book, the copyeditor noticed that a character had his shirt buttoned to the left in one illustration and to the right in another, that a round table on one page turned into a square one later on in the story, and that the windows of a house slid up and down in one illustration but opened outward in another. To spot such anomalies, the editor has to learn to look at illustrations in a different way, just as she has learned to scrutinize words differently.

In comparing illustrations with text in a story about a little girl who takes a walk along a beach, the editor noticed that the little girl was surrounded by her family in one picture, although no family was referred to in the text. In another picture, a starfish figured prominently among the child's finds on the beach but again received no mention in the text. In the first case, the editor persuaded the artist to eliminate the family from the picture; in the second, she persuaded the author to include the starfish in the text because the drawing was particularly appealing. As often happens, the editor acted as a mediator, in this instance resolving differences between the artist and the author.

Another challenge for children's book editors is working with a limited vocabulary: They must make sure the text is clear and coherent and the words used in any particular book are appropriate for the age group for which the book is intended. And because their readership is impressionable, they must be extra-sensitive to language and eliminate any trace of sexism, racism, ageism, or any other *-ism.* This is also of practical importance: Since schools and libraries are the principal markets for children's books, the language will be carefully scrutinized by the teachers and librarians who review them.

Because they handle illustrated books and deal with a variety of formats, children's book editors must have a thorough knowledge of production. It is their job to tell illustrators how the art should be prepared and what size it should be for the printer; they must know whether a photograph will reproduce well, how a particular color will print, what kind of paper is needed, how the pages should be laid out.

Finally—and perhaps most important—children's book editors need a special sense. An editorial director with years of experience expressed it like this: "Children's book editors have to know how a child thinks, talks, and sees the world. They don't have to have children of their own, but they have to know the child within themselves, and somehow be able to go back to that child."

What Makes a Good Children's Book Editor?
- A special sensibility toward children.
- A well-developed aesthetic sense for dealing with illustrations.
- An awareness of the right vocabulary levels.

47

- A heightened sense of responsibility toward readers (who are more likely than adults to be influenced by the books they read).
- A desire to entertain and educate.
- A sense of fun.
- An understanding of the production processes.
- The flexibility to handle a wide variety of books and give them all their due.

Checking It Out:
The Wide Wide World of Reference

Reference book publishing isn't what it was. Which is to say that, in recent years, it has changed beyond recognition.

Dictionaries and thesauruses, atlases and almanacs and encyclopedias still form the backbone of reference. But today the definition of a reference book goes far beyond these traditional products. To publishers, "reference book" has come to mean just about any book that provides information. Classified as reference may be books on popular history and politics, hobbies and sports, arts and crafts, nature and ecology; encyclopedias are available on a variety of subjects from baseball to popular science, from gardening to witchcraft; and, on the dictionary shelf in a large bookstore, you may find, in addition to the standard dictionaries, crossword puzzle dictionaries, sports dictionaries, rhyming dictionaries, dictionaries of eponyms, even a dictionary of Klingon, the planetary language spoken in the "Star Trek" TV series and movies.

Some publishers also classify as reference the enormously popular "self" books: the self-help, self-improvement, do-it-yourself manuals that tell you how to buy a used car, how to keep the love you've found, or keep off the weight you've lost. (So popular have these books become that the *New York Times* bestseller list has a special section for "Advice, How-to and Miscellaneous.") And in the rush to reference, children have not been left out. Reference books for young readers range from dictionaries and thesauruses to books on animals and nature, space and the environment.

Reference publishing used to be the bailiwick of specialized companies such as encyclopedia publishers or university presses. But as the reading public's appetite for information has grown, publishers of every stripe—from mass market to trade to children's books—have gotten into the act. Some leading trade publishers have set up separate reference divisions; others keep adding reference titles to their nonfiction lists, further blurring the line between reference and nonfiction.

For publishers, part of the appeal of reference books is that, unlike most trade books, many stay in print—on what's known as the publisher's backlist—for years. The initial cost can be high (developing a new dictionary or encyclopedia, for example, requires an enormous investment); but a dictionary or one-volume encyclopedia that becomes a classic will sell hundreds of thousands of copies over the years.

How do people get into reference publishing? Some decide at the start of their career that they want to work on reference books. But many others stumble into the field. We believe more editors would deliberately choose to work in reference if they had a clearer notion of what it entailed.

Let's confess first off that reference isn't glamorous. There are no author lunches, no blockbusters to brag about, no book auctions or publishing parties. But it isn't boring either, despite a rather general perception to the contrary. In fact, for anyone who is curious about how things work and about the world around us, it's among the most challenging areas of publishing. All editors learn from the books they work on; but *providing* information is at the heart of what reference editors do. In helping compile a biographical dictionary, for instance, the editor will rub shoulders with Charlemagne and Chagall, Hemingway and Hitler, Nefertiti and Nijinsky. In editing a yearbook, he or she will learn about such diverse matters as the mating habits of tree frogs, the worldwide obsession with soccer, or the most recent political crackdown in Myanmar (formerly Burma, as the books say).

All the same, it's fair to add that not all the material you'll deal with will be of equal interest; in editing a medical yearbook, you may be intrigued by an article on the latest high-tech scanning technology but less excited by a run-of-the-mill article on caring for your gums. You have to take them as they come and give each its due. Reference editing can also be frustrating and time-consuming since it demands infinite attention to detail and great assiduity in digging out information.

Reference editors need writing and organizational skills as well as editing skills because a lot of material has to be restructured or rewritten, and some material originates in-house. In books such as encyclopedias that have many contributors, final responsibility for the work rests with the publisher, not the authors. For editors that can be a source of satisfaction. As one senior editor put it, "In reference, editing constitutes value added to the final work. To me, it's more satisfying because it's hands-on, more of a creative process."

To get an idea of what traditional reference editing entails, let's take a closer look at encyclopedias, yearbooks, and dictionaries.

Encyclopedias and Yearbooks

An encyclopedia, according to *Merriam-Webster*, is "a work that contains information on all branches of knowledge or treats comprehensively a particular branch of knowledge." Encyclopedias on the market today range from the multivolume general encyclopedias used mainly by high school and college students to one-volume desk encyclopedias and specialized volumes on subjects such as history, science, and religion.

A yearbook is a supplement to a general encyclopedia, and its principal readership is encyclopedia owners. General yearbooks cover the year's events in major countries and regions of the world; they also include developments in the arts and sciences and humanities, business and industry, sports and entertainment. Specialized ones cover a particular field, such as sports, science, or health and medicine.

Preparing a complete revision of a major general encyclopedia is an enormous undertaking with a multimillion-dollar price tag. Indeed, the investment—in time, money, planning, editing, and production—is so great, and there is so much competition, that the appearance of a new encyclopedia or a completely new edition of an old one is a rare occurrence. New publications tend to be one-volume encyclopedias or specialized encyclopedias consisting of just a few volumes.

Today most publishers of general encyclopedias confine themselves to producing yearly revisions, in which a proportion of the material—somewhere in the area of 10 percent—is changed through updating existing articles and adding some new ones. This work requires a permanent staff, some of whom are generalists, others specialists in different areas—say, the sciences or the arts. Because an encyclopedia cannot expand indefinitely and old material usually has to be taken out to make room for new, deciding what to update each year is a difficult task in which considerations of cost, time, and available space all play a part.

Some changes *have* to be made no matter what. Wars, revolutions, and political upheavals such as the peaceful breakup of the Soviet Union and the bloody one in Yugoslavia must go in, as must the election of major world leaders, disasters such as a major oil spill or a devastating earthquake, and important events in sports and the arts.

Sometimes an addition has a ripple effect; when the Soviet Union broke up, encyclopedias had to add a separate article for each of the new republics; one encyclopedia also commissioned completely new articles on Josef Stalin and Leon Trotsky, as well as a major revision of the article on communism. And a new article on the Persian Gulf War made biographies of Colin Powell and Norman Schwarzkopf seem indispensable.

The need for some revisions is less obvious to the casual reader. Longstanding articles may suddenly become dated because of new cultural perspectives or new discoveries in science. One editor referred to articles on animals to illustrate both points. "Cultural attitudes toward animals have changed," he said. "When I was a kid, the questions one asked about animals were, What are they useful for? and Would they make good pets? We don't look at animals that way anymore. What we ask is, How do they fit into the natural world?"

And from the scientific viewpoint, an article on kangaroos had to be updated when the classification of these animals changed,[6] and one on shrews was redone when new data emerged on their life cycle.

In some instances, historical articles are affected by current events. For example, the cleaning and restoration of the Sistine Chapel ceiling, which was completed in 1990 and restored the colors to their original vibrancy, induced one encyclopedia not only to add full-color illustrations of the ceiling itself but to reevaluate Michelangelo with a new emphasis on his work as a colorist.

A common perception of encyclopedia work is that it is conducted by a group of scholars at a leisurely pace. The reality is quite different—each yearly revision is produced on tight deadlines, and as soon as one revision has gone to press (and often before), planning begins for the next one. Revising an encyclopedia is rather like painting a bridge: By the time you reach the end, it's time to go back to the beginning and start over.

Like trade book editors, encyclopedia editors are always on the lookout for new material; they read constantly—books and newspapers, technical journals and popular magazines—to keep up with current events or new scientific discoveries, or to identify likely candidates for a biographical article (not this year's celebrity, but a person who has made

---

[6] Kangaroos, which are placental mammals, were put into an "infra class" (lower than a subclass). It is now recognized that their placenta has its own singularity.

a mark in his or her field: a poet, novelist, or playwright, a scientist responsible for an important breakthrough).

Editors need to know as much about the past as the present—that is, have a broad education—because a large part of an encyclopedia deals with historical events. Most specialize in a particular subject area, say, the life sciences, the physical sciences, or the humanities.

Another part of the job is to acquire new contributors, both to replace old ones or to cover new topics. This means keeping up with the editor's field and knowing who the experts are. It may also mean getting to them ahead of the competition (other encyclopedias), particularly when the field is narrow and the experts are few. An example would be finding an expert to write an article on the former Soviet republic of Uzbekistan.

Reference editing is demanding work, but it can also be very rewarding. The editor in chief of a major general encyclopedia summed it up this way: "There's a certain satisfaction in giving information and trying to do it gracefully, making people want to read it, addressing them in an intelligent way, not treating them as inferiors. It's as if you were saying, 'Oh, you want to know about that? Then let me tell you about it.' And that's a very respectable human enterprise."

Editing a yearbook is much like editing an encyclopedia, except that a yearbook deals only with current events. Putting one together can be compared to putting out a newspaper—but a newspaper that covers an entire year.

Crunch time for yearbook editors comes in the final few months of the year. That's when articles flood in from hundreds of different authors, with a multitude of styles and wide variations in writing skills.

Senior editors on yearbooks have broad responsibilities. They must review articles for accuracy, clarity, and completeness, line edit them when necessary, and copyedit them to conform to an established overall style. At one general yearbook, staff editors, assisted by freelancers, work through the articles alphabetically from A to Z, reviewing them at several stages (manuscript, galley proofs, and page proofs). A deadline is set for finishing A to C articles, another for D to F, and so on all the way to Z. The end is in sight only when the articles on Zambia and Zimbabwe are ready for typesetting.

Besides the A-to-Z articles—the meat of the book—yearbooks generally include longer feature articles, which may be heavily illustrated and require special editorial care. Yearbooks also carry a list of obituaries of prominent people who died during the year. Putting this section together is a challenge, not the least because people keep on dying even as the deadline draws near and much juggling, cutting, and adding are required to make the copy fit into the space allotted.

Fact checking is a major part of the job. People read encyclopedias and yearbooks for *information,* and if the information in even one article is incorrect, readers may lose confidence in the entire book. And, although the authors' names go on the various articles, it is the publisher, not the author, who is held responsible for factual errors—and indeed for the final product.

Imagine for a moment that you are a new editor, a freelancer hired for the project, and you've been asked to fact check an article. If you're inexperienced, merely figuring out how to use various reference works—the *New York Times Index, Facts on File, Who's Who,* or *The Reader's Guide to Periodical Literature*—with their tiny print and mysterious abbreviations, will seem like a research project in itself. So will learning to use a computer database, or finding out whom to call for information. Knowing where to go for what—whether print source, database, government agency, university department, or corporate public relations department—is an acquired skill, and an important one, because editors are always working against the clock. Equally important is knowing what to check and what not to. It's impossible (as well as impractical, given time and cost limitations) to check every fact in every article. Editors learn through experience what must be done and what can be let go. If, for example, the facts an editor has checked in an article on a tiny African state have proved accurate, she won't spend an inordinate amount of time checking the spelling of the name of a minor government official. Editors also learn which authors they can trust and which ones have a reputation for being sloppy about verifying their facts.

A good reference editor enjoys research for its own sake. She thinks of herself as a detective doggedly pursuing every lead, going down every highway and byway, until she nails the elusive fact. No question seems too silly or too trivial to the good researcher. "Those trumpeter swan eggs you flew to Michigan in the spring," she says to a biologist. "Tell me, did they ever hatch?" When she succeeds in her quest, she gets that "Aha! Gotcha!" feeling. When she fails, she feels frustrated but makes the best of it, "fudging" when necessary, hedging a statement she can't confirm or sometimes even deleting it.

A good reference editor is effective on the phone; she has mastered the three P's—politeness, persuasiveness, and persistence. She is polite enough to make people disposed to help her; persuasive enough to coax an overburdened government official to go the extra mile (for example, to check the status of a bill pending in Congress) or to get a busy professor to update the economic statistics he sent in three months before; and persistent enough not to accept a vague or incomplete answer but to keep calling back—or asking questions—until she is satisfied.

At the senior level, the functions of encyclopedia and yearbook editors are extremely varied. They develop article ideas and acquire authors and are involved in every level of editing; they work with art and design staff to select illustrations; they do some final proofreading and checking, including page layout. And because a lot of judgment is involved, it's usually their job to "fit" an article into the space allotted, adding copy when necessary, deleting it to make room for last-minute changes.

A drawback for some is that they work on the same basic project year after year. (Encyclopedia departments do publish other books, but these tend to be one-time projects that account for just a small part of the workload.) On the other hand, the subject matter is varied, with much of it changing from year to year. And many editors thrive on the pressure of working under deadlines and producing a major work of reference in a seemingly impossible amount of time.

Dictionaries

Simply stated, the purpose of a dictionary is to describe words. Depending on its size and scope, a dictionary will define a word's different meanings, show how it is spelled and stressed and pronounced and how it is broken into syllables, explain where it comes from (its etymology), and list words related to it or close in meaning (synonyms). The description, or *definition*, may also include illustrative sentences or phrases that clarify a word's meaning by, so to speak, showing the word "in action."

Dictionaries vary not only in size and scope but in the readership for which they are intended. The most comprehensive are unabridged dictionaries, such as *Webster's Third New International Dictionary*. Probably the most widely used are the college dictionaries, which are of manageable size and useful as desk references. They include *American Heritage Dictionary* (3rd edition), *Merriam-Webster's Collegiate Dictionary* (10th edition), *Random House Webster's College Dictionary*, and *Webster's New World Dictionary* (3rd college edition) and are by far the bestselling dictionaries in the United States. Then there are bilingual dictionaries (such as French-English, English-French) and dictionaries for foreign learners (or ESL—English as a Second Language—dictionaries). There are also specialized dictionaries (in English) in subjects such as medicine, the law, and various branches of science, children's dictionaries for various age groups beginning with first readers, and many more. (We'll confine our discussion here to general, monolingual dictionaries.)

Perhaps the most illustrious of the unabridged dictionaries is the *Oxford English Dictionary*, which provides a history of every word it contains, going back to the word's earliest appearance in the language. The first edition of the *OED* was an extraordinary lexicographical achievement, particularly in a computerless age. First conceived of in 1857, the 12-volume work took 71 years to complete. The second edition, a mammoth of 20 volumes containing almost 60 million words, was published in 1989.

Some books that call themselves dictionaries are actually reference books; examples are biographical, political, and scientific dictionaries. At the same time, more and more reference material is appearing in dictionaries. Most college dictionaries, for example, include various kinds of general information, which may appear in the alphabetical list of words (the A-to-Z section) or else in separate sections, generally at the back of the book. Encyclopedic entries include names of people and places, Biblical books, titles of plays and songs, Greek gods, tables of weights and measures, metric conversion tables, mathematical signs and symbols, and so on. You may also find a section on style, usage, and grammar, or instructions on the correct way to address an admiral, an ambassador, or an alderman. Biographical and geographical entries offer readers a quick and convenient way of checking, say, the birth date of a Russian czar, the population of Thailand, or the capital of Togo.

Dictionary work calls for someone interested in words as words and comfortable working with small, discrete bits of text rather than articles or complete books. Some dictionary functions are specialized; the staff will probably include an etymologist and a pronunciation editor, as well as specialists who write definitions in their area of expertise. Other functions can be learned through experience; new editors often become definers with the help of some in-house training.

Defining—a major part of dictionary work—is difficult and demanding; it requires a broad general education, the ability to make fine discriminations, and above all a special feel for language. The definer must be able to write and to do so in a very particular way. She must define a word concisely, clearly, accurately, and without bias, leaving no doubt in the reader's mind as to its meaning. According to Sidney Landau, editorial director of Cambridge University Press, "Each definition . . . must constitute a tiny, discrete essay of its own, providing enough clues to context so that even in the briefest definition the readers know whether we are measuring fetuses or wavelengths, head sizes or reflexes."[7] (The statement was made in the context of a medical dictionary, but the concept applies to any type of defining.) The definer may also be asked to compose a phrase or sentence that illustrates the meaning of a word in a natural rather than stilted or strained context.

Dictionary editing requires intense attention to detail. While working with small units, editors must keep hundreds of things in mind. Each small piece connects with—and is affected by—everything else. Consistency is essential, and style rules must be rigorously followed. The style guide, which may run into hundreds of pages, is both bible and training guide, and it is consulted at every turn. (For a discussion of consistency, see Chapter 3.)

Consistency in dictionary work also means consistency of *approach*. For example, all the entries in a particular subject category—whether it is a large category such as biology, religion, or politics or a smaller one such as musical instruments, units of currency, or military ranks—must be reviewed to make sure they are treated in like fashion. Is a Buddhist defined in a similar manner as a Christian or a Muslim? Have political labels such as "conservative," "liberal," "radical," and "communist" been handled consistently? Is there a parallel approach in the biology entries?

One editor, given the "angels" entries to review, discovered there was a pecking order even in heaven. Angels were ranked in a celestial hierarchy of nine orders, with archangels near the top and cherubim and seraphim near the bottom. She was also asked to check on boxers, to make sure weight ranges were handled consistently; phoning various boxing associations, she got an education on the fine points

[7] Sidney I. Landau, *Dictionaries: The Art and Craft of Lexicography*. New York: Cambridge University Press, 1989, p. 145.

of bantamweights and featherweights as well as on the different rules governing boxing and wrestling.

Dictionary editors, as we've said, deal with small, discrete units. But those who run the project—generally an editor in chief assisted by a managing editor—must keep the whole picture in mind as well as its individual components. They will be involved to some degree in reviewing entries, in the choice of illustrations, tables, and charts, in decisions about which new words should go in and which old ones should come out, in working with the art director on the design, and in overseeing composition (typesetting). Content, design, and production are closely intertwined, and each affects the other.

This overview is intended to give a flavor of what dictionary editing entails. It is well to remember, though, that this is a very small field, and that dictionary editors are few in number. All the same, some of the qualities required to edit dictionaries are also needed in other kinds of reference work. For instance, the special kind of consistency referred to previously, which requires that all entries in a particular subject be treated in similar fashion, applies when dealing with entries in a biographical dictionary or any other dictionary of an encyclopedic type.

What Makes a Good Reference Editor?
- A broad-based general education.
- Curiosity about the world and an interest in knowledge for its own sake.
- A penchant for research.
- The ability to write well.
- Attentiveness to detail.
- The flexibility to work well with other editors.

The Sale's the Thing: College Textbooks

As we noted in Chapter 1, getting ahead as an editor usually means starting in an entry-level job such as editorial assistant and moving up. In textbooks, that's not the way to go. To become an acquiring editor in textbook publishing, you must travel a different road.

We mean that literally. Many acquiring editors (usually called acquisitions editors in textbook departments) begin their careers on the road as college travelers, otherwise known as sales reps. In textbook publishing, agents do not come to editors with books to sell. Book ideas very often originate with the publisher; travelers, many of them recent college graduates, go from one college campus to another, looking for book projects and prospective authors.

Textbook publishing is a competitive business in which the stakes can be very high. If adopted by many college departments, a book can sell many thousands of copies, go through several editions, and stay in print for many years. The risks, too, are high. Developing and producing a textbook generally requires a large investment of time and money. Most textbooks are printed in more than one color, and most have numerous illustrations, tables, and charts; many are part of a bigger package that may include ancillary materials such as workbooks, tests, and study guides.

Which is why it's critical to know the market. The acquiring editor must know what's going on in a particular field—say, economics, or mathematics, or the social sciences. With the help of college travelers, he must find answers to questions such as: What books are already out there? What are the current trends? What is the competition publishing? Is there a hole—a classroom need—my company can fill? If so, who are the prominent people in the field? Which of them might be willing to write a book to meet that need?

Once the traveler has come up with a promising idea and the names of possible authors, the acquiring editor generally takes over, persuading the author to write the book, helping decide its content, and negotiating the terms of the contract.

If it's a big book, a developmental editor (often a freelancer) may be assigned to work with the author, advising him or her on style, substance, and organization and perhaps getting involved with the writing itself. At some point in the process, part of the manuscript will be sent to reviewers—experts in the particular field—for suggestions and comments that the author must take into account.

Unlike trade editors, textbook editors rarely get involved in hands-on editing. They are hired because of their knowledge of at least one area of the marketplace. Their job is to be accountable for both the acquisition and sales of books in that area.

There are exceptions, though. One fairly small college division, which publishes about eighty books a year, hires acquisitions people with an editorial background as well as from the ranks of the sales reps. "We do a lot of English books," explained one senior staff member, "and we've found editorial people do better than the sales reps because they get more involved in the manuscript itself. Teachers acknowledge that our books are well edited—and teachers are always complaining that publishers don't care about the books, only about the money."

But although they don't generally edit, editors must know what features each book requires in order for it to sell. Should it be a four-color or a two-color book? What kind of illustrations—and how many—should it have? Does it need a glossary? A question-and-answer section at the back of each chapter or at the back of the book? Supplementary materials such as a study guide? Since all these decisions have financial implications, they are made in conjunction with sales and marketing staff—and often with the publisher as well.

The acquiring editor will be involved in other marketing decisions, including cover and jacket design. And since he will be held accountable for his sales projections, he will probably take a hand in selling his books to heads of college departments.

What happens to a textbook manuscript when it arrives at the publisher? It becomes the responsibility of an in-house editor—variously called project editor, production editor, or editing supervisor, depending on the house—who will see it through design, editing, and production. (In large textbook houses, editing, design, and production are often separate functions. In smaller ones, all or most of these functions may be handled by the project editor.)

A textbook manuscript requires a lot of preparatory work before it is ready to go into production. The project editor begins by reviewing the various elements: These may include several levels of heads, graphs, charts, and tables, numbered and unnumbered lists, extracts (long quotations set off from the text, usually in different type size), glossaries, footnotes, and bibliographies. The editor identifies any special problems and decides how to handle them, consulting with design and production staff. She may select sample pages for the designer to use when designing the book (although many publishers now use standardized designs). She makes decisions on editorial style, illustrating them with examples from the manuscript, and draws up a preliminary style sheet for the copyeditor, which may also go to the author for approval. (Consulting with the author at this early stage to clear up issues of both style and substance can often avoid problems later on.)

The project editor, like the acquiring editor, does no hands-on editing of the manuscript. Both copyediting and proofreading are sent out to freelancers; in some cases, copyeditors are asked to do line editing as well.

What's involved in copyediting a textbook? How does it differ from editing a novel, say, or a reference book?

Perhaps the biggest difference lies in the complexity of elements involved. Most novels consist mainly of straight text, with a minimum of headings, if any; reference books (excluding dictionaries) will have more heads, but these are likely to have a standard format throughout the book. A textbook copyeditor, on the other hand, has to deal with a sometimes bewildering variety of elements—and handle them consistently throughout the manuscript.

Column heads, rules, and abbreviations must be treated similarly in similar tables; the totals in columns of figures must be checked; percentages must add up to one hundred.

Footnotes and bibliography entries require meticulous attention: The editor must adhere to the publisher's style for punctuation, word order, and the use of italics and quotation marks. Cross-references to tables and illustrations must be checked to make sure they refer to the right item. And if the editor is required to code the manuscript for the typesetter, he must be familiar with complicated type specs and design.

Unlike reference editors, textbook copyeditors are *not* required to check facts, largely because expert reviewers have already done so. The accuracy of the manuscript is the author's responsibility. (They should, however, query if something sounds wrong or if they spot seeming contradictions or inconsistencies.) Neither should they tamper with the author's style as long as the meaning is clear. In textbooks, clarity is more important than elegance of expression.

Copyediting textbooks requires a solid educational background; specialized knowledge is not essential, except in the case of technical material such as advanced math, chemistry, or computer technology. Knowledge of a particular field may, however, give the editor an edge in getting work. And a good freelance copyeditor may well be considered for a staff opening when it comes. (For more on freelancing, see Chapter 6.)

What Makes a Good Textbook Acquisitions Editor?
- The willingness to travel, at least initially.
- A thorough knowledge of the market.
- The ability to promote and sell books.
- The ability to work with authors in helping shape their books.

What Makes a Good Textbook Copyeditor?
- The ability to handle complex material, such as tables, diagrams, and charts.
- A drive to get details right.
- An appreciation of the importance of consistency.
- A familiarity with design and typesetting specifications.

An Academic Environment:
The University Press

Do ivied walls have an appeal for you? Are you drawn to
the world of academia but not necessarily to teaching? If
so, you may find your niche in a university press.

University presses have a long history. The first one, Cambridge University Press, was established in England by royal
charter in 1534, but it took more than three centuries for the
first American university press to come into being. Today
there are more than a hundred of them in the United States,
in big cities, small towns, and rural backwaters—almost any-
where where there is a university. Presses come in all sizes:
The smallest may publish fewer than a dozen books a year,
the major ones several hundred. Although they are typically an integral part of the university to which they are
attached and will obviously give special attention to books
written by their own faculty, they publish books from many
sources and a variety of disciplines.

The goal of a university press is to serve the scholarly
community by disseminating new research or new thinking. Some commercial publishers or publishing divisions
also produce scholarly books. But unlike their commercial
counterparts, university presses are nonprofit and therefore
less constricted by the demands of the bottom line. As a
result they are willing to take on books that are of interest
only to small, highly specialized audiences and print them
in small quantities.

This does *not* mean that university presses don't care
about making money, only that market success is not the
only criterion in the decision to publish. A university press,
like any other publisher, hopes to come out ahead at the
end of the year or, at least, break even. Sometimes it can
offset the many books that are at best marginal with a few
perennial sellers (a desk encyclopedia, for example, or a
popular history series) or well-written, accessible books that
appeal to a general audience.

The editorial director of a major university press summarized its goals like this: "We're concerned with making ends meet, but we're more concerned with maintaining the quality and standards of our books. The reason for our existence is to serve the scholarly and academic community."

To maintain their high standards, university presses set up three major hurdles that each book manuscript or proposal must surmount before it is accepted for publication. The project must first get the approval of an acquiring editor, who then becomes its sponsor; it must then survive the scrutiny of two or more independent "referees"—usually experts in the particular field—who evaluate it and decide whether they think it is worth publishing. Even when the reviewers respond positively, they are likely to suggest some changes and revisions. After the author has made the changes in a satisfactory way (or offered convincing reasons why they should not be made), the project goes to a final arbiter—the faculty press committee, which must give its approval for publication.

The job of acquiring editors at a university press often combines the functions of an entrepreneur with those of a hands-on editor. Like textbook editors, they devote a major part of their time to sales; their "bosses" provide them with an office or a desk and, as one editor put it, "some money to set up shop and travel." And some, like trade book editors, help shape the manuscript and (in rare cases) do line editing as well.

Despite the scholarly environment in which they work, university press editors tend to be just as harried as their counterparts in other branches of publishing. Agents rarely knock on their door with book ideas (for one thing, royalties, and especially advances, are too low to make it worth their while), so editors must go out into the field and aggressively seek new projects. And, like other entrepreneurs, they are judged by their production—if not in dollars and cents, then by the number and quality of books they bring in.

Most acquiring editors focus on a particular field—say, English literature, economics, or another branch of the social sciences, although they don't necessarily have a degree in that field. Specialization allows them to become thoroughly familiar with the subject area and—equally important—to get to know key people whom they can turn to when they need peer reviews. An editor who develops a successful program in a particular discipline also helps build a reputation in that discipline for his or her publisher, and this reputation in turn attracts more good books.

Editors stay on top of their subjects in a variety of ways. They read professional journals, go to academic conventions, travel to campuses, and do a lot of networking. Talking to prominent scholars, seeking out the up-and-coming "stars," building links with the academic community—these are ways for editors to find out what individual scholars and their colleagues are working on. Being well informed will often give an editor the edge over the competition, whether in signing an important new book or acquiring an up-and-coming author.

Acquiring editors' in-house responsibilities include preparing catalog copy for sales conferences, answering query letters, and looking at unsolicited manuscripts (even though only a tiny percentage of these ever get published). And when one of his authors sends in a finished manuscript, the editor is responsible for reviewing it and preparing it for production, much as a textbook editor does. He or she makes sure that all the pieces are there, that permissions have been obtained, and that any special problems have been resolved before the manuscript is released; he also keeps track of the book's progress as it makes its way through production stages from manuscript to bound book.

The editor's job, though demanding, can be very satisfying to anyone with a love of learning. By having a hand in what's published in a chosen field, the university press editor can make a contribution to the advancement of scholarship in a subject he or she cares deeply about.

Where do acquiring editors come from? Some of them, like trade and reference editors, start at the entry level and work their way up. But at small presses—and most university presses *are* small—there aren't that many opportunities. Most houses prefer to promote from the inside, but it would be impracticable to jump an assistant editor with limited experience to the position of acquiring editor. More likely, the press would look outside for a more experienced editor to fill the slot.

The lesson for junior staff members who decide to stay in scholarly publishing is that, at some point in their career, they too may have to look outside the house in order to get ahead.

What Makes a Good University Press Editor?
A good editor:
- Has a broad-based education.
- Is intellectually curious.
- Can write well.
- Is aggressive and a self-starter.
- Has a thorough knowledge of his or her chosen field.
- Is comfortable in an academic environment.

Elementary and High School Publishing

School publishing, often referred to as el-hi, represents a huge segment of the book market in dollar terms, and a highly specialized one. Unlike other areas of publishing, it produces large programs rather than individual books. Most programs are developed as a series for several grades, with a pupil's edition and a teacher's edition for each grade as well as many supplementary materials: workbooks, study guides, tests, tapes, and so on.

Developing a new series requires an enormous investment of money, time, research, and editorial and production effort. It involves considerable risk as well as the potential for large profits. A series' being adopted by school authorities in major states (Texas, in particular) can lead to huge sales for the publisher. If the series fails to gain an adoption, the publisher may suffer considerable losses.

Like other areas of publishing, school publishing underwent major changes in the 1980s. As a result of mergers and acquisitions, some school divisions combined, and many smaller houses were swallowed up by larger ones or taken over by conglomerates. By the early 1990s, the number of major school publishers in the United States had shrunk to a handful. At the same time, in part because of the economic recession, local school district budgets were shrinking. As a result, school publishers cut back staff, and their editorial structure changed.

"The titles vary from house to house," says a supervising editor in a major publishing company, "but the structure is similar. A typical division has an editor in chief, who reports to the president or publisher at the top. In our house, beneath the editor in chief there's a director of each subject area, say, social studies or math. Below the director, there used to be several layers of editors. Now the staff is smaller and job distinctions have become blurred, because everybody does everything."

The distinction between elementary and high school texts has also blurred. Traditionally, elementary texts were for kindergarten through eighth grade, whereas high school books were for grades nine through twelve. Now high school divisions also produce books for the middle grades (six through eight). This means that in some cases, two divisions of the same house compete for middle grade students.

The Books and Their Publishers

School textbooks can be roughly divided into two main types: basic text programs (sometimes called "basals") and supplementary texts. Basic texts are large packages comprising a pupil book, a teacher's edition, and various ancillary materials. In a reading program, for instance, the ancillaries might include phonic and grammar workbooks, reading comprehension workbooks, and audiovisual material. Supplementary texts—usually individual paperback books or packages of booklets—are intended for use in conjunction with basic texts. Because they're not submitted for adoption, they don't have to contain the many elements usually required in basic texts.

Supplementary texts are generally produced by separate publishers, working with very small staffs. The ideas are developed in-house, but the books themselves are often produced by a packager. However, the lines between basic and supplementary texts are now blurring as well, as some supplementary publishers begin to move into basic texts and vice versa.

The Job of Schoolbook Editor

The concept for a new school program originates with the publishing house. It is developed, under the direction of the editor in chief, after research in the field, consultations with teachers and marketing staff and review of the competition, and consideration of the requirements (in terms of content, instructional materials, etc.) of states in which adoptions are coming up.

Once the concept is sufficiently developed, senior staff go out into the field and look for authors—for example, college professors, prominent educators, or theorists on the cutting edge. The publishing house also acquires a list of consultants, who will read preliminary material and comment on it. But, in general, although authors help develop the concept, neither they nor the consultants do much of the writing. That is mainly done by in-house editors.

The job of a schoolbook editor demands a broad range of skills. An editor working on a program is at various times writer, researcher, consultant, and proofreader. She must be familiar with book design and type specifications; she should have a feel for art and design and an in-depth knowledge of production; she needs computer skills. Ideally, she has a broad educational background as well as

a specialized knowledge of a particular field, be it literature, science, music, or social studies. She must also have
empathy with young people and a feel for what will engage their interest.

Let's look, for example, at the job of a supervising editor
in charge of a new reading program for grade 7. The editor
begins by looking for literature to use in the pupil's edition—a search that can take a year or more. Various genres
(e.g., fiction, nonfiction, poetry, biography) must be repre-
sented and must illustrate the broad themes that have been
chosen for the program; in addition, the material must be
multicultural and free of stereotypes and of course appropriate for the particular age group.

Once she has decided on the material and obtained the
necessary permissions, the editor writes instructional material to accompany each selection and works with the art
department on design and selection of illustrations. She
checks the artwork at each stage of production and makes
sure (just as children's and trade book editors do) that illustrations match the text and that they contain no trade names,
double entendres, or material that could be objectionable.
And she charts the course of the book through each stage of
production.

Perhaps even more demanding is the task of putting together the teacher's edition, which is done last, includes
a multitude of class activities and teaching strategies, and
may run to hundreds of pages. "There's never enough time,"
said one editor. "No matter what program I've worked on,
there's never been enough time left for the teacher's edition. You find yourself working seven days a week at the
end. Because you must make that adoptions date no matter
what."

Sometimes parts of the program are farmed out to a book
packager, but the editor is still responsible for the material
that comes back and may have to edit or even rewrite parts
of it. To complicate things further, the stages from manuscript to bound book overlap, with the result that the editor

may still be writing later sections of the teacher's edition while she is checking final pages for the earlier ones.

Because she has to keep track of so many different elements, the school editor must be more than knowledgeable and creative—she must, above all, be well organized.

Since school publishing is so highly specialized, we thought it useful to add a few words on getting into the field. As we noted earlier, school texts are now published by a very few large houses, nearly all located in or around big cities (mainly New York). In addition, there are jobs to be had with packagers and publishers of supplementary books, but both employ small staffs.

As in other areas of publishing, it's always possible for a recent college graduate (particularly an English major or someone with an education degree) to come in as an editorial assistant. Teachers who wish to switch fields are good candidates for a middle-level editing position; many school editors come from the ranks of teachers.

Freelancing is an excellent entree. Because staffs have been cut, publishers (and packagers) are using more and more freelancers, whose work is likely to be full-time and in-house for months at a time. And because the workload is usually heavy, a capable freelancer (say, a copyeditor or proofreader) looking for more responsibility has a good chance of getting it—and may also have a shot at a staff job when one comes up.

What Makes a Good Schoolbook Editor?
A good schoolbook editor:
- Has a broad-based education.
- Is a competent writer.
- Is computer literate.
- Has some knowledge of production.
- Has a feel for art and design.
- Handles pressure well.
- Is well organized.
- Has an empathy for young people and what interests them.

Other Publishing Areas

Other, highly specialized areas of publishing include professional books (books for higher education that are often multiauthor volumes, series, collections of essays, or reprints), Bibles and other religious books, and illustrated books (books on subjects such as painting, sculpture, photography, or architecture in which text and illustrations form an integrated whole, generally known as coffee-table books).

A Foot in the Door

What do editors look for in hiring an editorial assistant? The basic skills listed in the want ads at the beginning of this chapter—typing or word processing, organizational ability, attention to detail, a good phone manner—are pretty typical requirements. In addition, editors look beyond those requirements for talents and skills that suggest the applicant has the potential to make a career in editing.

Editors we spoke to in many different areas of publishing emphasized the importance of a liberal arts education (a B.A. degree is a minimum requirement), a love of reading, and a basic command of language and grammar. They judged language skills in various ways. "If there are ungrammatical sentences or typos in the cover letter," a reference editor commented, "I know this person is not for us." An editor in mass-market fiction looks for someone with "an excellent eye. I ask them to read a paragraph and pick out the typos. If they can't spot them, they're not going to make good proofreaders. I might also ask an applicant to read a chapter and then write a little bit about it, because being able to express yourself is an important part of the job."

Editors also agreed on the importance of being well organized. In publishing, every step of the book's life—beginning even before the contract is signed—is carefully documented. A record is kept of every stage of production, and the important task of keeping the record straight is often the responsibility of the editorial assistant.

Editors in different fields have additional requirements. One college textbook editor feels that some knowledge of typesetting and production, however elementary, is indispensable. "I would ask a job applicant, What is a pica? What is a running head? What is a folio? Or I'd ask them to name one method of composition, any method."

Editors also look for candidates with an affinity for the kinds of books the editors are publishing. The editorial director of a university press wants an applicant to be "intellectually engaged" in some area of learning; an editor of romance novels won't hire anyone who doesn't enjoy reading romances. "You have to like a particular genre in order to be any good at acquiring it," she said, "because ultimately editors are readers. And in choosing books, they have to trust their instincts."

"Edit the kind of books you like" may well be the single best piece of advice to anyone contemplating an editing career. There is no surer way to be happy in that career.

Several editors cited willingness as an attribute they look for. Willingness may not seem terribly important to candidates, who are probably fantasizing about the contribution they're going to make to the world of books. But editors value it because it makes their job so much easier. "I look for absolute willingness," an editorial director in children's books stressed, "to do just about everything that has to be done—xeroxing, filing, folding book jackets for sales conferences, getting packets ready for sales reps, answering the phone. All of that is necessary. Then, on the job, the person will begin to see what it is we do when we edit."

Being willing not only helps your employer, it helps your career. Doing anything and everything except watering the plants or making the coffee (unless it's your turn) is the best way to learn what is going on. We'll elaborate on this in the following section.

Getting Ahead

By now you may have formed the impression that the job of editorial assistant is a thankless one. It's true that at the beginning, at least, you'll be doing mostly routine work—and being poorly paid for it.

Remember, though, that at most publishers the job is considered an apprenticeship, a way to learn the editing trade—and that's the way to approach it. We emphasize "learn" because the process will be mostly do-it-yourself; in a busy editing department no one will have much time to teach you.

The editorial assistant has a perfect vantage point from which to observe the workings of a publishing house. As liaison between the editors you're apprenticed to and other departments, you have the chance to familiarize yourself with the editorial and production process. Sitting in at editorial meetings—where you may be asked to take the minutes—you'll get a lesson not only on the process of manuscript selection but on the economic factors involved in the decision to publish.

You also learn by looking at everything that crosses your desk: the author correspondence you're given for filing, the contracts you're asked to send out, the copyeditor's or proofreader's corrections you input on the computer, the permissions you must request. Take note of how editors formulate author queries, of the kinds of changes they make on manuscripts, of how little or how much editing was done in each case.

Reading "slush"—the unsolicited manuscripts that every publishing house receives in large quantities—presents another opportunity for the editorial assistant. (Today many publishers send such manuscripts back unread, believing that the time and cost required to uncover a worthwhile project are not justifiable; others, particularly in category fiction, still take a look at them.)

Eager beginners always hope to find true gold buried in the slush pile. Be warned that one rarely does. But reading slush and writing reports gives would-be editors a chance to demonstrate their literary judgment and show off their writing skills.

As an editorial assistant, you should also be willing to learn new skills. Learn to use the computer even if it's not required; study proofreaders' marks on your own; offer to write jacket copy if it's not part of your job. And consider taking a publishing or editing course on your own time. The interplay between theory and practice can be invaluable, and some publishers will pay all or at least part of the tab if the course is job related.

And don't miss the opportunity to (tactfully) pick any brains in sight. An editorial director in textbook publishing recommends finding out what your colleagues are up to, what the adjoining departments are up to. "And get yourself a few mentors," he added, "at least one of whom is in production."

"Keep your eyes and ears open and just be a sponge," says a recently promoted editorial assistant. "But also keep your own vision of what you like and what you believe in, because when you get to be an editor, you have to rely on your own instincts."

You may decide after a few months that an editing career isn't for you. It's too nitpicking, too detail oriented, too poorly paid. In that case, it's time to consider your options, which include a complete change of profession or a move to a different area of publishing. Switching to a different publishing job—say, production, publicity, marketing, or subsidiary rights—shouldn't be too difficult at this early stage in your career, particularly if you're working in a big house and have made some contacts. In a smaller house, though, there'll be fewer opportunities to switch from one area to another, and you may have to look for a job in a different company.

If you do stay in editing, the good news is that it is by and large a meritocracy. If you do your job well, you'll probably be promoted. We'd be remiss, though, if we didn't point out the enormous role chance plays in getting ahead. Because publishing is such a fluid business, and moving around so common, being in the right place at the right time is often the crucial factor.

We've seen a raw young editorial assistant take two quick steps up the ladder in a matter of months because others moved on; we've also seen talented senior editors remain in their jobs year after year, getting raises but no promotions, because there was no place for them to go.

But until the opportunity presents itself, you have to pay your dues by going through the apprenticeship. And you have to *care*. As one editor put it, "Since the money isn't good, you must do it for love."

Chapter 3

Principles to Edit By

The intellectual challenge is always there, but more than anything else, editing is fun—so much fun that it's easy to get carried away.

—Mary Stoughton[1]

Editing itself is an excruciating act of self-discipline, mind-reading, and stable cleaning. If it seems like a pleasure, something is probably wrong.

—Arthur Plotnik[2]

You're an editorial assistant in a mass-market publishing house who has been on the job for nine months. You're a junior member of an encyclopedia department who has recently been promoted to assistant editor. You're a freelance proofreader who has passed a copyediting test. The three of you have one thing in common. You have just been given your first manuscript to edit.

Your assignments are somewhat different, and so are your instructions. You, the editorial assistant, have been told to line edit a mystery novel; you, the assistant editor, have been handed an article for an encyclopedia yearbook on the year's highlights in television and given free rein to do "whatever needs to be done" with it. You, the freelance proofreader who aspires to be a copyeditor, have had a short manuscript

---

[1] Mary Stoughton, *Substance & Style: Instruction and Practice in Copyediting*. Alexandria, Va.: Editorial Experts, 1989, p. 2.

[2] Arthur Plotnik, *The Elements of Editing: A Modern Guide for Editors and Journalists*. New York: Macmillan, 1982, p. 34.

entitled *Ten Easy Ways to Improve Your Self-Image* delivered to your door with a note saying that all it needs is "a little light line editing."

All three of you have done your homework. The editorial assistant has gleaned nuggets of editing wisdom from her boss by reading his scrawled pencil comments in the margins of manuscripts and by carefully studying his queries to authors. She has also taught herself the copyediting symbols. And, whenever time allowed, she has looked through the copyeditor's changes and queries before shipping manuscripts to the authors for review.

The assistant editor has been equally assiduous. He read the senior editors' query letters to authors when copying them for the file and paid attention to changes in manuscripts as he keyboarded them on the computer, comparing them with the author's original version. He has occasionally been asked to do some fact checking, which has impressed on him the importance of accuracy in reference books intended for the record.

The freelance proofreader has prepared herself to copyedit while going about her own work. Checking the changes made by copyeditors, she has asked herself how she would have handled that particular sentence or phrased that particular query. In addition to spotting typos, she has kept an eye open for stylistic inconsistencies; occasionally, she has discovered a plot discrepancy and brought it to the attention of the managing editor, who told her she had "a good eye." Encouraged by this praise, she recently took a copyediting test and passed it. She wants to copyedit for the higher pay but also for the satisfaction of doing hands-on work on a manuscript.

Each of you is self-educated as an editor. You've received no formal in-house training, been given no overall guidelines, had no books in the field recommended to you. What you do have, as you sit down at your desk, are *The Chicago Manual of Style*[3] and *Merriam-Webster's Collegiate Dictionary*

[3] *The Chicago Manual of Style*, 14th ed. Chicago: University of Chicago Press, 1993.

(10th edition) (or whatever style guide and dictionary your publisher uses), your college copy of *The Elements of Style*,[4] perhaps a house style sheet—and your boss's airy invitation to "ask if you have any questions."

You were excited when you were first given the assignment. But as you sit down and glance through the manuscript for the first time, at home or in the office, you suddenly feel intimidated, even overwhelmed. Until now, every manuscript that crossed your desk had already been edited: Words had been deleted, others inserted above the lines; colored flags were attached to many pages. Now, for the first time, you're facing a virgin manuscript—and that gives you pause. Dare you, you wonder, pencil in hand, sully those pristine pages? Skimming through, you spot an adjective that sounds a little strange, a grammatical construction that seems clumsy. But can you—should you—change those things? Can you *really* make the book "better"?

You've been told to feel free to ask questions, but you hesitate to keep running in and out of your boss's office (or to call him several times on the phone), fearing you will look ignorant. (In fact, most bosses prefer you to ask some questions up front—it saves a lot of time later redoing things.)

It may help you to remember that a new manuscript can seem daunting even to the experienced editor. There is no pat formula, no one way of approaching each different text. Each book has its own problems; each feels like starting from scratch. Once you overcome your panic, you'll probably take your supervisor's advice and "plunge right in," which is the time-honored way editors have learned their craft.

We believe there is a better way.

In Chapter 1, we described the various stages of the editing process: the cutting and shaping, the rewording and clarifying, the nuts-and-bolts work of correcting style, grammar, and usage. What new editors lack, however, is an underpinning, a conceptual framework that will inform every

[4] William Strunk Jr. and E. B. White, *The Elements of Style*, 3rd ed., with index. New York: Macmillan, 1979.

editing decision and help them perform these essential tasks.

In this chapter we provide that framework, distilling our philosophy of editing into a set of guiding principles and providing examples of how to put them into practice.

Experienced editors—if they are any good—will, through a process of trial and error, have developed a conceptual framework for themselves, even if only subconsciously. We hope that, for them, our principles may serve as a reminder, and also as a teaching tool.

For the beginner, the guidelines will make it easier to break down the task at hand and evaluate what—and how much—has to be done. They will also give her a sense of security and let her pick up her pencil with confidence—which is as important to the job of editing as experience and expertise.

A writer fond of describing editors as "book doctors" had this advice for his colleagues: "Some editors are surgeons, others are butchers. Be sure you get one with a scalpel, not a hacksaw. And above all, don't let some quack give you the wrong medicine!"

As "book doctors," editors should take to heart the old medical maxim—and make it the bedrock of their editing practice:

First, do no harm.

Editors can do harm primarily in two ways: when they alter an author's individual style—her voice—or when they change the content or meaning of her prose.

Doing no harm when editing a manuscript means doing the minimum necessary to clarify an author's language or intent, which is also the essence of our first principle—economy.

Principle: Economy

Virginia Woolf was once advised by her father, essayist and editor Sir Leslie Stephen, "Say as much as you can in as few words as possible." If all writers followed this advice, there would be very little to edit. Fortunately, or unfortunately, many of them don't, leaving plenty of work for editors. Stephen's advice works for editors too. Good editing, like good writing, should be *economical*.

HOW-TO:

Change as little as possible to correct a sentence or make it intelligible

A novice editor in particular may find it easier and less time-consuming to rewrite a sentence than to attempt to "fix" it. By fixing a sentence we mean making an author's meaning clear while retaining as much of the original language as possible.

All too often, rewriting is an editor's attempt to make sense of an ambiguous sentence or phrase. The result may be a sentence that is "clear," but one that also changes the author's intent. Sometimes the point of a sentence is buried in an awkward phrase or an odd grammatical construction. With practice, an editor will be able to pinpoint the intended meaning and clarify it as nearly as possible in the author's own language. The key to fixing a sentence is to know exactly what the author is trying to say. If there is any doubt as to the author's meaning, the editor should simply query.

Obviously, there are times when sentences, paragraphs, even whole pages have to be redone from scratch. Ideally, the responsibility for such major rewrites should be the author's. If this is not feasible and the editor must rewrite, she should do so in a style that conforms as closely as possible to the author's (and whenever possible, clear the rewrites with the author).

Editing is one craft to which the adage "less is more" applies. Yet the single most common mistake line editors and copyeditors make is to do too much. Why? New editors, anxious to prove to their superiors that they have mastered the minutiae of grammar and usage, tend to overedit. But so, at times, do experienced editors, perhaps in an effort to validate the importance of their own function, or simply out of a failure to grasp what a writer is trying to accomplish.

For example, in a short story about urban life, a writer described a fireman standing on the landing of her building as "wielding an ax." The editor changed the verb to "holding," saying that was what the firefighter was actually doing. Literally, he was correct. But his choice of verb was not only dull ("hefting" would have been better), it also lost the effect the writer was aiming for—humor through exaggeration. The image of a ferocious fireman wielding an ax cooing "Nice kitty" to the protagonist's cat (as he did in the next paragraph) was substantially weakened by changing that one word. Such "minor" alterations can also compromise the rhythm and flow of a sentence.

In another instance, an editor changed the title of a nonfiction piece to be included in a collection of essays from "Winter in Israel" to "Israel in Winter," which she no doubt did in the name of clarity. The author was livid. His essay, a powerful evocation of Israel's winter of discontent as the *intifada* (the Palestinian uprising) began, now sounded like a travel piece. His first-person account had ended: "For now, even as spring approaches, it is still winter in Israel," a metaphor obviously lost on the editor.

Use of the passive voice is perhaps the stylistic device most out of fashion with today's editors, who prefer the clarity and punch of the active. But as the following example from a medical textbook article on liver transplants shows, an editor should never follow a rule slavishly.

AU.: "By the spring of that year, three additional transplants of this type had been performed successfully."

ED.: "By the spring of that year, doctors had successfully performed three additional transplants of this type."

The edited version is less good because the focus of the sentence was on the *transplants*, not on who did them. Also, "doctors" (contributed by the editor) adds a note of vagueness. The transplants would obviously have been done by surgeons.

Don't adjust an author's style, or language, simply for the sake of changing it—because it's not to your taste

In other words, if it ain't broke, don't fix it. And *don't* edit that favorite old saw to read "if it isn't broken, do not fix it"!

Gratuitous editing and unnecessary rewriting are the most common complaints writers make about editors. And justifiably so. The editor's job is to allow the author's voice to emerge without coloring it, or replacing it with her own. An editor who wants to write should be a writer.

The following simple examples illustrate the principle of economy.

AU.: "There is many a noble man to be found in the kingdom."

ED. 1: "Many a noble man can be found in the kingdom."

ED. 2: "Many noble men can be found in the kingdom."

Ed. 1's change simplifies the sentence. But Ed. 2 has altered the slightly archaic tone the author intended. (Would you change "Once upon a time" to "Years ago" just because it's more concise?)

AU.: "The great German composer Richard Wagner, who was short, had a wife who was tall, which earned him derision."

ED. 1: "A short man, the great German composer Richard Wagner had a tall wife, which earned him derision."

ED. 2: "The great German composer Richard Wagner, who was short, had a tall wife, which earned him derision."

By eliminating one of the clauses, Ed. 2 has improved the sentence's flow. But Ed. 1, by shifting a phrase, has also shifted the emphasis from Wagner's greatness to his height—not the author's intent.

In trade book editing, economy does not necessarily mean making sentences shorter or more concise. For example, in one novel, sentences were long, with many clauses woven together, to give the feel of old-fashioned writing, of a rush of storytelling, like Dickens's or Trollope's (and quite unlike Hemingway's tight, short prose). The editor respected the author's style, breaking long sentences only when they were a tangle and making sure that nothing misread.

In reference editing, where space is almost always at a premium, economy is critical. In a biographical dictionary slated to contain about 15,000 short profiles, the goal was to make each entry as interesting and informative as possible within the space allotted. Difficult choices had to be made about what to put in and what to leave out. There was no room for wordiness; conciseness was more important than the style of each individual entry. Compare these two versions:

AU.: "Gore, Albert, Jr. (1948–) Vice-President of the US, born in Washington. After graduating from Harvard in 1969, he attended Vanderbilt University in Tennessee, studying at the divinity school and later its law school."

ED.: "Gore, Albert, Jr. (1948–) US Vice-President, born in Washington, and educated at Harvard and at Vanderbilt, where he studied law and theology."

In the second version, the editor has managed to save quite a few words without sacrificing much information.

A good way to describe an editor's function is to compare him or her to a baseball umpire. The best umps, like the best editors, are invariably the ones you don't notice. They guide the game but don't intrude on it. They "let the players play."

Principle: Tact

According to *Merriam-Webster*, "tact" derives from *tactus*, the past participle of the Latin verb *tangere*, meaning to touch. Great quarterbacks are often described as having "touch"—the ability to throw a football accurately and for distance so that it lands gently in a receiver's hands. Great editors can be said to have touch—a light touch when editing a manuscript, and a gentle touch when dealing with authors. These two aspects of editorial touch are what we mean when we talk about an editor having tact.

Skip an entry in *Webster's* and you find "tactic," defined as "a device for accomplishing an end." Tact is simply the best tactic an editor can use to bring an author around to his point of view on a manuscript—a viewpoint that ideally reflects not the editor's ego but his conviction of what is best for the book. The derivation of tactic (from the Greek *taktike*) has military connotations, reflected in its second meaning, "a method of employing forces in combat." But an editor's tactic is to *avoid* hostility, to ensure that the author/editor collaboration remains exactly that and does not become confrontational.

A writer's receptivity to suggestions may well depend on how tactfully the editor presents them. That being so, all editors, as well as proofreaders, must learn the art of the tactful query.

HOW-TO:
*Express your queries clearly, concisely,
and respectfully*

Respect, clarity, and conciseness—these are the essential ingredients in an effective editorial query. An editor has to be able to communicate her own ideas *clearly* and show that she grasps exactly what an author is trying to accomplish. Queries must be *concise* and to the point, even if there are only a few of them. All authors—not just those new to the editing process—are apt to be put off by queries that more closely resemble dissertations. An editor should not show off her knowledge or expertise; she should use it to make *pertinent* suggestions on a manuscript.

We emphasize "respectfully" because mutual respect is at the core of the author/editor relationship. Respect creates trust and should permeate every aspect of an editor's dealing with an author. An author trusts an editor who

85

"sees" his work as he does, who shares his vision of what it should be and shows respect for his language and ideas. To keep that trust, she must demonstrate complete understanding of—and empathy for—the author's purpose.

Let's look at a querying example. A tense political thriller set in Cold War Berlin has a long digression describing the Nazi era. The author regards this as essential background, but the editor feels that it interrupts the novel's action and slows the pace. Instead of saying, "This passage is boring and unnecessary. Cut!" the tactful editor explains, "Your plot is tight and fast-paced; this lengthy descriptive passage breaks the tension and may lose the reader—OK to cut?" If the author insists on keeping the information, an alternative suggestion might be to use the description elsewhere, perhaps incorporating it into a flashback dealing with a character's childhood (which would be more in the fictional mode of showing, not telling).

This example illustrates several points of good query technique: (1) An editor should praise an author's work before criticizing it, especially when the criticism is major (i.e., one calling for cuts or reshaping). (2) Any suggested change should be in the best interest of the book and not just reflect the editor's personal taste. (3) The phrasing of the query is vital. For instance, the editor does not say that the passage "will put the reader to sleep" but that it "may lose the reader." "May" (or "might") is a word that softens an editor's assessment. "Perhaps," "in my view," and "sometimes" are other examples of tactful phrasing. To communicate effectively, an editor should be diplomatic, not aggressive or overbearing (which is why the editor asks "OK to cut?" rather than commanding "Cut!"). (4) When possible, especially when suggesting a major change, an editor should be prepared to offer the author an alternative. Even if the change is a minor one, it can help the author to have choices. For instance, a copyeditor didn't merely note that "enormous" appeared several times in the same paragraph; she suggested that one be deleted as redundant and another be replaced with "vast."

Another example: In an article for a medical yearbook, an author cites a figure of 25,000 for the number of new cases of postpolio syndrome in a given period. The editor, in fact checking, finds the figure is grossly incorrect. Instead of bluntly telling the author, "Your figure is wrong," she might phrase her query: "There seems to be a discrepancy here. The *Journal of the American Medical Association* [date, page] cites a figure of around 18,000, and the *New England Journal of Medicine* [date, page] has 17,500. Please reconcile."

Here the editor uses tact to make the correction without embarrassing the author. Note the use of "seems to"—a very useful expression in sparing authors' feelings—as well as "please" and the request to "advise," seemingly leaving it up to the author to make the actual correction. Also, the editor has been very specific about the *sources* of her information—in reference editing, especially, a must.

General editors usually relay their questions to authors in a letter or on a query sheet (see Chapter 5, Figure 5.1). Copyeditors generally write their questions on flags affixed to manuscript pages. Often, copyeditors come across passages whose meaning is unclear, and they flag the manuscript: "Au. please clarify." It is more useful to indicate *in what way* the writing is unclear; perhaps information is missing or an ambiguous word choice has muddled the meaning. Since the author wrote the sentence, it's probably clear to him. You, the editor, may have to gently persuade him why it doesn't "seem" clear to you.

Here's another tip offered by a passionately committed copyeditor: "Don't be afraid to query if your editor's already suggested something to the author that's been shot down. Ask it in a different way or keep wearing the author down on the same point. If you're proofreading, the same applies. By about the third time they're asked, authors sometimes realize there's a problem. Also, the further the author gets away from the act of writing, the more likely he is ready to accept emendation."

Many editors will tell you that the better the writer, the more he or she appreciates intelligent editing. And many writers say that the best editors are the ones who are toughest (but tactfully tough, we hasten to add!). Nevertheless, it is up to the author to accept or reject editorial changes. It is the author's book—his name and his name alone appears on the title page—and he has the last word. And he may even be right.

An editor who does prevail after many a heated discussion with the author, and whose viewpoint is validated by great reviews, should resist the temptation to say "I told you so." She must be content to have been associated with a book she can be proud of and not expect recognition from the author.

Sometimes an editor gets lucky, though. Like the one who edited so tactfully that she received the following note from a so-called difficult author: "Your suggestions were so subtle, so delicately phrased and intelligent, that I took them gladly, convinced that they must be my own ideas."

Principle: Flexibility

Editors are seen as the arbiters of taste, style, and usage, but good editors cannot be arbitrary. They must be *flexible*. Essentially what this means is that they *listen:* They never fail to take into account an author's feelings. If an author has a reasonable suggestion as to what should be done for her book—from the jacket art to the choice of a freelance copyeditor—it should at least be considered, and not rejected out of hand. Conversely, any reasonable author will take an editor's suggestions seriously. Her trust is a by-product of respect for her editor.

A flexible editor has a far greater chance than a rigid one of ensuring that his interaction with a writer does not become adversarial. This is not to say that the editor/author interchange can't be lively or that it won't, at times, be heated. But it is up to the editor to monitor the debate and maintain its reasonable tone—and to compromise when necessary.

Principles to Edit By

Take every manuscript you edit on its own terms

Editors must be flexible when giving a manuscript its first read and evaluating its overall structure and tone. No two books have the same editing needs; therefore, there's no set formula to follow.

Let's compare two nonfiction books that were written in a similar style. One was a case study of a schizophrenic patient; the other, the autobiography of a Hall of Fame pitcher. Both authors liberally used sentence fragments in place of complete sentences with a subject and a predicate, a style that is not wrong (it is used all the time in everyday speech and informal language) but that in excess can become tedious.

Some examples from the case-study book:

"She got up from the chair. And watched the doctor. Then smoothed her dress. Her favorite dress, the blue one."

In the opinion of the editor involved, the style was too casual for a book that, though intended for a general audience, was scientifically based. In working through the manuscript, he made judgments about when subjects should be added, when phrases should be run together into sentences, and when they could be left, for variety or emphasis.

On the other hand, the "fragment" approach worked well for the sports book, which was an engaging monologue, written in an easy conversational style. The book's appeal was that the author was talking directly to *you*, spinning baseball yarns over a beer. The editor's decision was to let the sentence fragments stand except where they created confusion as to who was meant or what happened.

It comes down to a question of balance—and of editorial judgment. A good editor remembers that he is a reader too. If a particular style or word usage bores or irritates him, it will probably do the same to the audience.

Flexibility is essential when editing fiction. For instance, a young adult novel told from the mind of a poorly educated thirteen-year-old girl cannot be made rigidly grammatical. If she thinks "If I was rich . . ." (instead of "If I were rich . . .") or says "He don't know no better" (instead of "He doesn't know any better"), her loose, colloquial language should be left intact. (Of course, this does not apply to grammatical errors so egregious that they compromise the meaning.)

Editing so-called literary fiction demands the most flexibility because, even more than usual, an editor has to adapt his sensibility to the author's and make sure he does not stifle the author's voice. This often means letting stand quirks in style, usage, and grammar that would be unacceptable elsewhere.

Take the example of a writer whose first language wasn't English, but who wrote an almost poetic, if occasionally confused, English. The editor was careful to query any garbled sentences, and any phrasing that could be misread. He was also attentive to word choice, making sure that a word had the meaning the author seemed to want. (When, for example, the writer used "outhouse" to mean "outside shed," the editor had to explain diplomatically that in American English an outhouse usually means a privy and ask for a substitute.) But the editor did not attempt to rewrite the author's language or to make it conform to standard usage.

In the words of one "flexible" editor: "The English language allows for many different styles of writing. Allow the author his."

The principle of flexibility applies mainly to editing trade books. In reference books, for instance, it is more important to establish a consistent style for the book as a whole than to retain the flavor of each contributor's writing.

HOW-TO:
*Bring a fresh, open (literally!) eye
to every book you edit*

So far, we've discussed flexibility in the context of the overall approach to a manuscript. The principle is equally important in the process of copyediting—a point that beginning editors especially should take note of. They should also note that the previous sentence ends in a preposition.

"Never end a sentence with a preposition" is but one of the "taboos, bugbears, and outmoded rules of English usage" that Theodore M. Bernstein debunks in *Miss Thistlebottom's Hobgoblins*.[5] Bertha Thistlebottom—the archetypal prissy, fussy grammarian—epitomizes what every editor should not be: a language autocrat.

Ironically, new editors are in special danger of becoming language autocrats. In their desire to be "right," novices sometimes fail to leaven adherence to the rules of grammar and usage with simple common sense.

The passive voice is generally weaker than the active and, as we've seen, is currently out of vogue with editors. But one copyeditor went so far as to change *all* the passive constructions in a manuscript, ignoring the niceties of stylistic variation and also changing the meaning of some sentences by shifting the emphasis.

Another copyeditor went on a "which" hunt. In the biography she was editing, she changed every "which" used in a restrictive relative clause to "that." For example, "This is the symphony which he wrote for his wife" became "This is the symphony *that* he wrote for his wife." Technically this is correct usage. But English is flexible, and today varying "whiches" and "thats" is widely accepted.

The copyeditor also failed to consider the sound of the language she altered. In the preceding example, the author's use of "which" produces an alliterative effect that was weakened by the change to "that." (In the previous sentence, "which was weakened" would be inferior to "that was weakened" because the sound of three consecutive words beginning with a "w" is less pleasing to the ear.)

Miss Thistlebottom would have been proud of these two language autocrats, graduates of the "I have learned a rule and I will apply it" school of copyediting. They would have

[5] Theodore M. Bernstein, *Miss Thistlebottom's Hobgoblins*. New York: Farrar, Straus & Giroux, 1991.

done better to have heeded the succinct advice of one copy chief to her staff: "Think twice; restrain yourself."

Obviously a mastery of "correct" grammar and "standard" usage is indispensable to good editing. But experienced editors add another element to their education: Through reading and listening they learn to appreciate that English is a living, changing language, not one whose rules are carved in stone.

Principle: Consistency

Consistency and flexibility are two sides of the same coin. An editor has to be able to tell which is called for when. The ability to make this distinction is largely the result of experience, developing a good ear, and knowing the fine points of the language.

Consistency is not maintained for its own sake, but to aid the reader. Its function is to enhance readability and help make the author's intent clear. The principle applies to style and usage as well as to details of plot and characterization.

As they strive for consistency, copyeditors and proofreaders must themselves be consistent.

HOW-TO:
If you make a style decision, stick to it

A basic editing tenet is that it is better to be consistently "wrong" than inconsistently "right." For example, you may have decided to hyphenate "copy-editor" throughout a manuscript, even though current American usage leans toward making it two words. Although others may disagree with your choice, hyphenating the word consistently is preferable to doing it in some instances and not in others. Or perhaps you would choose, as we have, to make "copyeditor" one word. (Our thinking was that since "copyedit" is one word according to *Webster's*, "copyeditor" should be too.)

While flexibility is especially important in editing fiction, consistency is vital to editing every kind of book. "[Consistency] can hold together a less than superior piece that has substance, and it can add polish to a really fine piece."[6]

For instance, an economics text replete with figures must have a standardized number style (e.g., spell out numbers under ten; use 6 percent in text, 6% in tables; no commas in four-digit numbers: 1050, not 1,050). Encyclopedias have style "bibles" to ensure consistency among the hundreds of entries written by different authors. The compilers of such style guides must resolve issues such as the following: Abbreviate United States to U.S., US, or USA?; use "premier" or "prime minister"?; capitalize or lowercase ("Premier" or "premier")?; use Great Britain, the United Kingdom, or the British Isles? Without such a detailed style guide, the overall effect of a variety of inconsistent usages would prove very distracting to readers.

Gross inconsistencies in a book not only confuse a reader, they diminish the credibility of both the writer and the publisher. Could you take seriously a pregnant heroine who married in August and had the baby the following July, as a blizzard raged outside? Would you trust the veracity of that author's subsequent account of his protagonist's trip down the Amazon?

A young adult book featuring kids slogging through the rain forests of Borneo had three contradictory descriptions of the way tattooing was done by native peoples. Would you accept the accuracy of any other tidbit of local lore the author presented in that book?

One key to consistency is the editorial read, which is discussed in detail in Chapter 4. Editors read to remember. Which means paying attention and knowing what to look for. Good editors also know that it is virtually impossible to catch *all* style inconsistencies the first time around. A final, quick read is needed to catch any stragglers.

[6] Mary J. Scroggins, "Editorial Consistency Enhances Readability," in Mary Stoughton, *Substance and Style: Instruction and Practice in Copyediting.* Alexandria, Va.: Editorial Experts, 1989, p. 328.

Also covered in Chapter 4 is the style sheet, an invaluable aid to maintaining consistency. It serves as a memory jog for the copyeditor as well as a guide for the proofreader.

Keep in mind that corrections in galley or page proofs can be costly

In their zeal to make a book as nearly perfect as possible, editors are tempted to make changes up to the last minute. But at this stage, costs must be kept in mind. Although the typesetter pays for printer's errors (PEs), such as typos, the publisher absorbs at least some of the cost of author's alterations (AAs). The publisher also bears all of the expense of editor's alterations (EAs). (If EAs are over the limit set by the publisher, the in-house editor may be asked for an explanation.)

Attention to consistency at the copyediting stage can minimize the number of errors that appear on the printed page. It also saves the publisher money and makes it easier to meet publishing schedules.

Editors must also be consistent in the *level* of editing they decide on. Editing is commonly classified as "heavy," "moderate," or "light" (although those terms may mean somewhat different things to different editors). New editors are often inconsistent in their level of editing. Many an enthusiastic novice starts out editing too much, too slowly, and then has to speed through the manuscript to meet a deadline. Pace is important in editing, and the ability to pace oneself comes only with experience. A quick overall read before putting pencil to paper will help the beginner get a feel of what the manuscript requires.

During her initial read of a manuscript, an acquiring editor will generally decide how much editing is needed. Once the level has been established, it should, if possible, be maintained consistently throughout the book.

If, for example, you are assigned a manuscript slated for

light editing, don't get carried away in the middle and start polishing every sentence. You may, of course, come across a bad patch—an abrupt switch in tone or a particularly unconvincing piece of dialogue. In such a case, it's reasonable to make an exception. But if, after a quick read, you feel a manuscript needs more extensive editing than you've been asked to do (say, it's been marked for "moderate" and you think "heavy" is what's needed), it's advisable to alert your boss right away. For one thing, heavy editing will take more time. For another, your boss may disagree—and explain why.

Finally, with consistency as with anything else, it's possible to have too much of a good thing. Consistency must be tempered by common sense. In the words of Ralph Waldo Emerson, "A foolish consistency is the hobgoblin of little minds." Emerson was taking a crack at "little statesmen and philosophers and divines." He might equally have addressed his warning to editors and proofreaders.

Principle: Confidence

In any field one has to have confidence in order to be successful. Having professional confidence is largely the result of "knowing yourself," to paraphrase the Greek philosopher Socrates, who, if he'd been a job counselor, no doubt would have also advised, "Know your stuff."

For acquiring editors, this means keeping up to date in everything from industry trends to current events. For copyeditors, it means constantly polishing their craft and adding to their general knowledge.

So, given that our editors know their stuff, what role does confidence play in their applying it?

For the acquiring editor, confidence has special importance in two areas: in choosing his projects and in developing them with his authors. Knowing what will sell is not an exact science. An editor can't choose his books on the basis of what was previously (or even what's currently) successful because chances are that last year's bestseller—a "woman in danger" thriller that every house rushed to publish its own version of—will be next year's flop. Of course, an editor has to have an instinct for what will sell; but he must also have confidence in his own judgment—a confidence that allows him to take risks, to go out on a limb for a book he believes in.

Every writer, whether she's working on the Great American Novel or updating an anthropology textbook, wants (and should have) an editor's confidence.

An editor who believes in a writer's work and who demonstrates it through his support and enthusiasm is the greatest single asset an author can have—and may even be pivotal to that writer's career. An editor's confidence will very often raise the writing to another level by encouraging a writer to believe in herself, which, for many writers, is the greatest struggle of all.

The editor's nurturing role also has practical advantages. Maintaining his confidence in a book even when the author becomes discouraged may tip the balance and ensure that the book gets finished—and even turned in on time.

Line editors and copyeditors are also confident in their own ability and are able to project that confidence onto the edited page.

HOW-TO:
Press firmly on the colored pencil

The first rule when marking up a manuscript is *don't be tentative*.

Among the many new recruits we have trained was a young man who insisted on using a No. 2 black pencil, which is harder to read than a red pencil. Eventually it became clear that this editor was so insecure about his changes that he was trying to make them as inconspicuous as possible. A little nagging and some additional experience convinced him that it was important to stand by his judgments—and to switch to a red pencil.

Tentativeness is understandable in beginners. But editors who lack confidence soon lose the confidence of both writers and colleagues. As an editor, you have to be willing to assume responsibility and make decisions. That's what you've been hired to do. So edit with confidence even when you're not completely sure of yourself. Remember, editing is very subjective, and no one can be 100 percent sure.

HOW-TO:
Write legibly and neatly

In editing, neatness counts. Make your corrections neatly and clearly; think them out before you write to avoid a lot of crossing out and erasing. You should use standard editing marks (which can be found in *The Chicago Manual* and in other standard copyediting manuals; see "Annotated Bibliography" in Chapter 8) and indicate your changes and additions above the line, not below.

Copyeditors especially should do as little rewriting as possible on the manuscript itself (unless given specific instructions to the contrary). Instead, they should use flags to query the author and also to write out their suggested major changes. A messy manuscript with hard-to-read changes implies a careless attitude on the part of the editor. An author who gets back a manuscript in such a condition may well lose confidence in the editor—and be less receptive to the suggested changes.

Editors require a long apprenticeship, and confidence develops slowly. Learning to "press firmly on the colored pencil" comes from practice and from paying attention to the nuances of every manuscript.

"So how can I edit confidently if I have no experience?" we hear a nervous new editor ask. It isn't easy, but take heart. Chapter 8 recommends a wide variety of self-help books, from copyediting texts to self-teaching manuals. It also lists editing courses and publishing programs that can increase the confidence of the aspiring copyeditor and jump-start her career.

Principle: Respect

A key theme of this book is: Treat all authors, and their work, with respect. We reiterate it here as a principle because we believe it can't be stressed enough. By "respect," we also mean an editor's self-respect, the pride that motivates her to do her job—particularly the job of editing a manuscript—well.

More specifically, this principle means that an editor should respect the style and content of a writer's work and should edit every book to the best of her ability. In theory, this seems obvious; in reality, it is easier said than done.

Every editor dreams of working on a first-rate book—a fine literary novel, an important biography, or a ground-breaking book in a scientific field. But such projects come rarely; most books, like most writers, are average, and some are mediocre, at least in terms of the writing.

It is well to remind oneself that many books are bought not for the quality of their writing but for their commercial potential. A tell-all autobiography of a famous rock star is likely to sell no matter how poorly written—and it may be assigned more publishing time and attention than a brilliant first novel by an unknown writer. Frustrating as this may be to an editor who loves good writing (and what editor doesn't?), it is still her responsibility to do the best job she can—within the limits of the material and the time available—when assigned a book that is less than a masterpiece. In other words, every book deserves its due.

As "book doctors," editors should learn to develop a clinical attitude toward books they don't personally respond to and give them the same professional care and attention as books they love. Occasionally, though, a freelance editor finds a book so problematic that he feels compelled to turn it back to the in-house contact.

An editorial consultant, himself an environmental activist, was hired to line edit a manuscript that debunked as "myths" even the most widely accepted environmental concerns. From the book's tone, he surmised that the authors wouldn't be amenable to suggestions aimed at presenting a more balanced view. So he declined the project, concerned that his own bias would prevent him from giving the book its due. In another instance, a freelance copyeditor received a novel to edit that turned out to be a sadomasochistic "love" story that she personally found repugnant. She finished the assignment as conscientiously as possible. She did, however, ask the production editor who farmed out work to spare her such books in the future.

Showing *respect* to a difficult author can sometimes seem too much to ask. Authors can be demanding, dense, or downright exasperating. At one extreme are the ones who are so protective of their work that they reject out of hand even the smallest changes; at the other are those who seem willing to divorce themselves from their writing once they have delivered the manuscript, abdicating to the editor responsibilities that are rightly theirs. These are the authors who send in manuscripts full of typos, with dog-eared and coffee-stained pages, with material missing, or with inadequately researched information. (Fortunately, the majority of authors fall between these two extremes.)

HOW-TO:
Take pride in your work, remembering
that every book you edit
is a reflection of your professional skill

So what's an overworked, underpaid editor to do when faced with a difficult or careless author? In rare cases, an editor may decide not to publish a manuscript—for example, when the author has failed to meet agreed-on conditions regarding length, content, approach, and so on. Or, if a book is part of a series and can't be replaced in time, the editor may go ahead and publish it but decide not to work with that particular author again.

Unfortunately, there is no magic solution for dealing with "problem" authors. All you can do is grit your teeth and remind yourself that giving respect to an author usually results in getting it in return. At the least, it will help create a smooth working relationship. And, if you are patient, your respect may even persuade the author to see things your way and agree to make changes that will improve the book.

Principle: Responsibility

As we've seen, different editors have differing responsibilities, and each contributes in a different way to making a book its best possible self. A major concern of an acquiring editor is to make the book salable; a line editor wants it to be clear and well written; a copyeditor, consistent and factually correct.

Editors also have different constituents to whom they are responsible. A senior trade book editor is responsible to the publisher he works for (representing his house during contract negotiations), to the author (acting as her in-house advocate), and to the specific audience for which he is acquiring (giving that audience what it wants, whether it's a "bodice ripper" romance, a legume cookbook, or a "definitive" biography of Madonna).

While a trade book editor's first responsibility is to the author, a reference editor's primary allegiance is to the book itself. With the reading public in mind, the reference editor must make sure the work is as accurate, objective, informative, and complete as possible.

Line editors and copyeditors also represent the book-buying public. Reading on behalf of a book's potential audience, they are responsible for making sure that—in terms of credibility and clarity, at least—a book, whether a spy thriller or a sociology text, is worth the asking price. Ultimately they are responsible to their employer and must meet each publisher's requirements on every manuscript they edit.

Finally, every editor, in every job and area of publishing, is responsible to himself or herself.

HOW-TO:
As an editor, you have to want to do a good job for yourself

What we're talking about here is simple, old-fashioned caring. Editors of every stripe, and for that matter most publishing professionals, lament that that's what's missing today, not only in editing but in bookmaking in general.

Blame for lack of caring is liberally distributed. Editors in chief claim that the conglomerates that own most publishing houses care only about the bottom line. Senior editors claim copyeditors don't care about editing, line editors say writers don't care about writing, and copyeditors—the last in line and much maligned—are sure nobody cares about books but they. Lack of time and low editorial pay are also cited as culprits. So, given all the excuses, why *should* you edit care-fully today?

The answer is simple. You do it for your own self-respect. Respect is the corollary of responsibility; together they make the "two R's" of good editing. If you care about every book you edit, you will fulfill your responsibility to author, publisher, and public—and also to yourself.

Chapter 4

The Editor's Senses

The five senses—sight, hearing, smell, taste, and feel—can all be said to play a part in the editing process. Editors with an "accurate eye" and an "ear for language" are valued by colleagues and writers alike. An editor who consistently spots bestsellers is said to have a "nose" for the market, while one with a talent for bringing out the best in authors has a "feel" for writing. And editors who sample a portion of a finished manuscript to ensure that it is up to standard are indulging in copy "tasting."

In this chapter we use "senses" to mean the special faculties every editing professional must develop in order to be effective. Among them are the editor's "eye," "ear," "nose," and common sense.

Editing is not—or shouldn't be—done in a vacuum. Ideally, editors start out with a set of general principles or basic assumptions (the kind we have articulated in Chapter 3) as well as a thorough knowledge of grammar, usage, and style. As we see it, the editor's senses serve as the vital link between principle and practice. (While all editors need to develop these special faculties, our main focus in this chapter is on the line editor and the copyeditor.)

Our discussion of how the editor's senses work in practice is not intended to provide answers to the many specific questions of usage, style, and grammar that editors confront every day. That is not the main focus of this book. (The annotated bibliography in Chapter 8 provides a list of resources that can help resolve such questions.) Our intention is to give readers a feel for what it takes to be an editor and for the editing process itself.

The Editorial Read

Before getting into a discussion of the individual senses, let's take a look at how editors approach a new manuscript—how they set the stage. Although, as we saw in Chapter 2, different kinds of editors edit differently, almost all begin with the *editorial read*.

Senior editors often read a manuscript through once without touching it to get an overall sense of its structure, organization, and language, and also to determine the level of editing it needs. The level of editing required is largely determined by the quality of the writing, but the type of book, its length, its importance to the publisher, and the demands of the schedule all play a role in the decision.

If he passes the project to a junior associate or copyeditor for line editing, the senior editor will usually instruct her to do a light, medium, or heavy edit. The heavier the edit, the more time it takes, and it is up to the editor to pace herself so as to maintain a consistent level of editing. This can be difficult, especially if the manuscript is long and the deadline is short.

There are no hard and fast rules on how to do an editorial read—or, indeed, on how many times an editor needs to go through a manuscript. Each editor has a different method; each finds out through experience what works best for him or her. The point, for one editor, is to read as any reader would, sitting on her hands if necessary. "I try to come to the manuscript fresh, to be as objective as possible, to let it work on me and not vice versa." Another editor also has the reader in mind. "What the reader wants is to feel satisfied by the book he plunked down $25 for. So I use the first read to ask myself this question: Has the book fulfilled its promise? If it was supposed to entertain, I want to feel amused; if it was supposed to inspire, I want to feel uplifted; if it was supposed to terrify, I want to feel frightened. My job is to give the reader his money's worth."

A closer, more detailed second read, which the editor does with pencil in hand, is generally used for line editing and to vet the editor's previous impressions. The things that jumped out at him during the first read may seem less important the second time around, and he may decide to leave them alone. Alternatively, problems of tone, characterization, and so on may turn out to be more serious than he originally thought. This read is used to check for everything from structural weaknesses to details such as an author's individual word choice.

Most senior editors stress the importance of doing a first and second read. But some find one read sufficient to gain both an overview and a line-by-line sense of a manuscript— and can't help picking up a pencil.

Copyeditors, too, have their own variations on how to read, and edit, a manuscript. The consensus seems to be that, ideally, a copyeditor should read a manuscript through three times—always with red pencil poised. The first read is designed to catch mistakes in spelling and grammar as well as to establish a consistent style. Line editing, if any, is generally reserved for the second read. "I leave a lot of things loose, until I get the rhythm and know the author's pattern," says one copyeditor. The second read may also function as an "overall" read, which a copyeditor uses, as a senior editor does, to validate her initial responses.

The third read—the "loose ends" read—is used to pick up what was missed in the first two, as well as to make sure that the content is coherent, transitions work, and the writing flows. This is also the read where the copyeditor ascertains that her editing marks are clear, her writing is legible, and any flags that are no longer relevant have been removed.

Reading a manuscript three times is the ideal. But in reality, time and cost restrictions often intervene, and the second and third reads are usually combined into one. One copyeditor doesn't always do a complete second read, particularly if the author knows what he's doing and there are few problems. Which doesn't mean she reads each sentence only once. She may read some of them as many as five times. Another copyeditor "flies through a manuscript the first time just to get the feel of it," then settles down to do a careful edit.

Whatever the method used, the final read is the one where the editor edits and proofreads herself. This means checking that her changes fit smoothly into the manuscript and do not disturb its flow. It also means making sure that no errors have been introduced. The worst sin an editor can commit is to take out something right and replace it with something wrong.

One tool every copyeditor uses is the *style sheet*. Figure 4.1 is an example of a nonfiction style sheet (an abbreviated version of our own); Figure 4.2 is a style sheet (also abbreviated) used in editing a mystery novel. Style sheets are detailed, alphabetically arranged lists of words compiled by the copyeditor to establish consistency and ensure that house style is followed. Copyeditors use them as a reminder when they come across variant forms (e.g., *traveling* or *travelling*, *the bishop* or *the Bishop*, 6 A.M. [small caps] or six a.m.); proofreaders follow them to avoid inconsistencies. Any word with a variant spelling or that could be easily misspelled should be added to the style sheet, as should some hyphenated and compound words. Place names as well as proper names (discussed in the next section) fall into this category, as do foreign words and phrases.

The copyeditor compiles the bulk of the style sheet during her first read, though she usually fine-tunes it later. Most trade houses do not blindly follow *The Chicago Manual* or *Merriam-Webster* (or any other style guide or dictionary) but give the author leeway; and the house style, if any, often follows the preferences of the chief copyeditor, who may lean toward hyphenating prefixes or capitalizing "Communist." Style sheets for reference books and textbooks conform more rigorously to house rules but also on occasion take account of an author's style or spelling preferences.

In addition to points of style, fiction copyeditors often

Sharpe and Gunther: EDITING FACT AND FICTION: A CONCISE GUIDE
TO BOOK EDITING

General

Use serial comma in list of three or more items:
editor, author, and publisher

Use italics for defining a word (first mention only), for
foreign words or phrases, and for emphasis:
    the term _database_ means . . .
    the past participle of the Latin verb _tangere_
this book does _not_ deal with printing and production

Use quotes for words referred to as words:
the word "editor" has a multitude of meanings

In general, use "author" in preference to "writer" in the
context of publishing:
    the author/editor relationship
    the contract between publisher and author
    but: a brilliant and accomplished writer of mystery novels

Spelling, Hyphenation, and Capitalization

backlist (n., adj., v.)   hands-on (adj.)
bestseller, bestselling   hotline
copyedit, copyediting,   in-house (adj., adv.)
 copyeditor, but line   nitty-gritty (n., adj.)
 editor   paperbound
disk (not diskette)   pop-up (adj.)
editor in chief (not   proofread, proofreader
 editor-in-chief)   sci-fi (adj., n.)
fax (n., v.), not FAX or sourcebook
 Fax   typeface

Numbers and Abbreviations

Spell numbers one hundred and under:
    a group of four editors
a staff of 112 people

Generally use figures for units of measure:
5 inches, 10 percent, 30 miles

Use numerals for time:
    2 _P.M._, 4 _A.M._ (small caps)
but three o'clock in the afternoon

Note the following forms for dates:
    2500 _B.C._, _A.D._ 94 (small caps)
    May 1994 (no comma), May 29, 1994; the 1940s, the forties

Figure 4.1

keep lists of characters—their names, ages, any personal characteristics (e.g., the color of their eyes, the make of their car, where they went to school), as well as how they interrelate with other characters (see Figure 4.2). This may seem excessive, but it's amazing how often authors confuse the details of their own creations. Keeping "character" lists, while time-consuming, often proves a lot more efficient in the long run than having to go back through a manuscript trying to find earlier references. One editor even keeps track of the chronology of a novel; for example, if the novel's time span is a two-week vacation, she lists events and codes them according to "day one," "day two," and so on.

Memory

As an editor, you read in a completely different way. *You read to remember.* If you enjoy and learn something as well, consider that a bonus. Obviously, it's impossible to remember everything you read in a manuscript and too time-consuming to jot down on a style sheet every descriptive detail or allusion to a time or place. Which is why every editor needs to develop that special "memory," that selective sense of what to look for—and what to retain—when reading a manuscript.

As with most editing skills, this selective sense is developed largely through experience. Let's say a problem pops up late in a manuscript, perhaps an inconsistency in plot or characterization, or a contradiction of a previous statement. A seasoned editor will probably remember earlier references and be able to put his hands on them quickly. He can then flag the inconsistencies and refer them to the author for clarification. The editor, if he thinks certain items are going to be "trouble," may include page numbers when compiling a style sheet.

Reading to remember helps the editor spot all sorts of textual discrepancies. Some of the most common are:

CAPITOL CRIME by F. B. I. Wiggins

<u>General Style Points</u>

No serial comma

Nonrestrictive that/which: both OK, follow au's style

Use italics for
  periodicals (Washington <u>Post</u>, <u>Fortune</u>)
  movies (<u>Gone with the Wind</u>)
  misc. (<u>American Gothic</u> [painting], <u>Normandie</u> [ship])

Use quotes (roman) for song titles ("Hail to the Chief")

Style for possessives: McGinniss's, Lewis's

Numbers:
      Follow au's style, e.g., fifty percent; but numbers
in dialogue OK (make consistent within sentence, paragraph).

<u>Spelling, Hyphenation, and Capitalization</u>

<u>A-B</u>	<u>E-F</u>
afterwards	eighteenth century
alright	eighteenth-century (adj.)
antilynching	eyeing
bedclothes	F.B.I.
blond (adj.)	F.D.R.
blonde (n.)	farfetched
<u>C-D</u>	<u>G-H</u>
canceled	G-string
cliche	German-American Bund
counselor	goddamn
	godammit
Daddy (direct address)	grande dame (roman)
but my daddy	
Democratic Party,	halfway
but the party	health insurance (adj.)
	homicide division

Figure 4.2

Character Summaries

<u>Lawrence "Bud" Stone</u>: F.B.I. agent in charge of
investigation of Senator Vecchio's death; fiftyish, stocky,
balding; bespectacled, rather bland appearance belies keen
intelligence; health food addict and hypochondriac;
divorced, with one son.

<u>Senator Dilworth McHugh</u>: longtime Republican Senator,
Washington power broker; mid-60s, very tall, well built,
distinguished-looking, with exceptionally large, pale white
hands; longtime personal and political foe of murder victim
Democratic Senator John Vecchio, who was strangled in the
Senate Cloak Room.

<u>Charlotte McHugh</u>: wife of Senator McHugh, a good 20 years
his junior; slender, intense, blond; her passions are chain-
smoking and gardening; favors basic black, fine gold
jewelry; hates the Washington scene; rumored to have been
romantically involved with the murdered senator.

<u>Lincoln "Linc" Jefferson Brown</u>: African-American D.C.
homicide detective; early 30s, sharp-tongued, cynical about
politicians; drives a green vintage VW bug; plays tennis
left-handed, hates baseball and rap music; highly
competitive with Bud Stone.

Figure 4.2 (*cont.*)

Time warps. Almost everyone knows what a "whodunit" is. The copyeditor quickly becomes familiar with another genre that could be called a "when-was-it."

Fiction writers sometimes seem confused about the chronologies of their stories. Was the murder committed at 4:30 P.M. or 4:30 A.M.? Were the spies supposed to meet at twelve midnight or twelve noon? Did the heroine disappear in the morning or early afternoon? On June 4 or June 5? Was the trek up the mountain supposed to take three weeks or two, and did the native bearer fall to his death on Day 5 or Day 7 of the expedition?

It may not be crucial to the plot that an internationally renowned diva (who happens to be a spy) sings *Tosca* at La Scala on Tuesday, after the author originally scheduled her for Wednesday. What *does* matter is the impression that a pattern of inconsistency (even in seemingly insignificant details) makes on the reader. In short, consistency helps strengthen any book's credibility; inconsistency weakens it and may even destroy it altogether. At the very least, inconsistencies are a distraction: No reader wants to waste a moment wondering how a time bomb supposedly set to explode at 4:42 reset itself to detonate at 4:45.

Nonfiction writers aren't immune to time warps either. In a book on ancient sculpture, a writer repeatedly mixed up his B.C.s and his A.D.s, leaving the reader confused about the century being discussed. And the author of a college history text used C.E. and B.C.E. ("of the common era" and "before the common era," respectively) at the beginning of the book, then abruptly switched to the more familiar A.D. and B.C. midway through.

"How can writers be so careless?" you ask. There are as many reasons as there are writers. Some are indifferent, others are working against tight deadlines. Some are just plain sloppy. Most authors do proof their work, but, as every editor knows, it's tough to catch all the mistakes in a manuscript you're overly familiar with. It is also the rare author—whether of fiction or of a scholarly work—who bothers to keep as thorough a chronology as a careful copyeditor does.

Descriptive indiscretions.   Writers can be merciless. One novelist killed off the same character twice, first of a heart attack on page 31, then from cancer on page 74. For good measure, "Lottie's fatal heart attack" was again referred to on page 142! In a "men's adventure," *Bessie*, "a stalwart little seaplane," which crashed at the end of Chapter 3, miraculously revived and was again delivering the mail in Chapter 5. Twin sisters Leslie and Jane were introduced early on as minor characters in a mystery. By page 53, Leslie had become Jane's twin brother, creating a mystery in itself.

In these instances, the discrepancies were relatively obvious. Tougher to catch is the obscure or seemingly meaningless inconsistency—for example, the one time a character who had been described as always wearing three-inch heels appeared wearing flats.

"It's so trivial," you say. "Why bother?" As a copyeditor, you can't always be sure what's important and what's not. The woman with the heels, for instance, was the subject of a profile in a psychological case study. The author, a psychiatrist, was delighted that the editor caught the discrepancy, explaining that the sudden change in heel heights would have belied his portrait of a rigid and controlling woman, completely set in her ways.

For the copyeditor, the moral is, flag anything that's suspect, even if it seems silly. And don't feel silly doing it!

Sometimes an author's "descriptive indiscretions" seem more comic than disastrous. It was with uncanny ease that a character described as left-handed used scissors in her right hand to dispatch her husband. A woman dancing in a blue dress in one paragraph suddenly found herself cha-cha-ing in red in the next. And a pet dachshund named Max metamorphosed into a poodle three chapters later.

Mistakes of any kind, even small ones, compromise the integrity of a book. When a reader catches the author out in even one mistake, the author's credibility is lessened. Your job, as copyeditor, is to ensure that descriptive details such as those mentioned here are consistent and make sense in context.

Improper names.   What's in a name? A copyeditor would probably say "spelling mistakes and inconsistencies and even other names." The "name bane" afflicts both fiction and nonfiction.

In fiction especially, names have a way of mysteriously changing. In a family saga, Aunt Beulah became Aunt Bertha and was eventually known as "our beloved Beebe." As Bertha, she also had a nickname, "Bertie," so credit for consistency should be given to the author for at least starting every name with "B."

To be fair, such inconsistencies aren't always so capricious. Midway through a manuscript an author might have seen that the names of two characters were too similar (e.g., John and Jack; Andrews and Anderson) and decided to change one of them. In so doing she could easily miss a couple, even if a computer was used to make a global search and change each mention of the name. Sometimes it's the copyeditor who points out confusing similarities of names (and he should always be on the lookout for them).

Variations in the spelling of names in nonfiction are often a matter of style. One copyeditor opted for Dostoyevsky over Dostoevski and Tolstoy over Tolstoi in a Russian literature textbook where both forms were used. (If, however, "Tolstoi" appeared in a title or a quotation from previously published material, the spelling would be retained.)

It is often helpful to keep a name list, particularly for a manuscript that includes many names. The list serves as a memory jog by providing a running account of the names and the pages on which they appear. If the editor suspects that a particular name was spelled differently earlier in the manuscript, she has only to refer to her list to check her hunch. It should be noted that proper names also include place names, for example, of countries and cities, seas, rivers, and mountain ranges; a separate list should be kept for these if necessary.

The name list also helps ease "copyeditor's anxiety," a syndrome that manifests itself in such questions as, Have I caught every last "Straus" (in a biography of waltz king Johann Strauss)?; How many acute accents have I missed (on Mallarmé, the French poet)?; and, Is this really the first "Da" (in Leonardo da Vinci) with a capital "D" that I've come across?

The Editor's Eye

In ordinary reading, errors are often missed because the eye automatically corrects a familiar word that is misspelled or jumps over a word incorrectly repeated, say, "of" at the end of one line and again at the beginning of the next. Experience and training teach editors to see mistakes that the average reader usually overlooks. The editor's special way of reading—his "eye"—enables him to see that something on the page is wrong, even if he doesn't immediately know how to correct it. The "mechanical" eye is the eye for details of form and style; the "perceiving" eye focuses on subtleties of sense and logic. Both of these "eyes" can be trained and improved upon with practice.

The "Mechanical" Eye

This "eye" is what every proofreader needs to proofread accurately and thoroughly. It reads word for word, even letter for letter, instead of scanning the lines as we do in ordinary reading. It catches the most easy-to-miss typographical errors, such as dropped quotation marks, single instead of double quotation marks, or vice versa, and copyediting oversights such as spelling mistakes and style inconsistencies. The eye checks to see that the compositor has followed the copyeditor's instructions in setting such things as foot-notes, quotations, and tables. It also makes sure the basic design specifications are met, for instance, that a main head is on a separate line, or a subhead is in italics, with the text run in. ("The 'Perceiving' Eye," below, is an example of a main head; "Anomalies" is an example of a subhead.)

Copyeditors also need their mechanical eye to spot typos in the manuscript. But it's the proofreader's responsibility to pick up errors in galleys or page proofs that copyeditors and compositors have missed.

The "Perceiving" Eye

This is the eye that detects anomalies, anachronisms, and breaks in logic, which are extremely easy to miss. Here are some actual examples.

Anomalies. Smoke is described as "curling out of a fire-place" in a novel that took place in midsummer. Unless the novel is set in England, or in some other place where the midsummer temperature might be 50 degrees, this state-ment is worth querying. Just ask, "Why a fire in July?"

Cicadas are described as "singing in April." Cicadas, at least in Pennsylvania, where this novel took place, normally sing in the heat of summer. A simple "Would cicadas be singing in April?" is sufficient.

A "tough, canny" big-game hunter sets off on safari in the African bush to track "the elusive and exquisite snow leopard." The problem is that the snow leopard inhabits Central Asia, *not* Africa. The average copyeditor wouldn't necessarily know such a fact, but she should certainly check it. A tactful query might suggest replacing the snow leop-ard with some other big game.

Sometimes a perfectly reasonable explanation for an anomaly emerges later in the manuscript. For instance, the smoke caused by that fire in July could have been the result of a villain's desperately trying to cover up his misdeeds by burning secret documents. And the early-singing cicadas might have turned out to be the signal of some sort of environmental disruption. In such cases, the copyeditor should remove the query flags as soon as the discovery is made—they're too easy to miss later.

One way for copyeditors to approach anomalies is to see them as pieces in a "What's Wrong with This Picture?" puzzle. A quick pass over such a puzzle will reveal obvious incongruities, such as a dog with a squirrel's tail. But only the careful eye will pick out more subtle disparities, such as a King of Hearts playing card printed with the Queen's picture on it. Your prize, as a copyeditor, is a sense of professional satisfaction—and perhaps the thanks of a grateful author or senior editor. For when anomalies such as these make their way into print, a reviewer is certain to spot them—and to complain of careless writing and sloppy editing.

Anachronisms. A character sings "I Love Paris" to herself in a romance novel set in the 1930s. We have nothing against singing heroines; the problem here is that "I Love Paris," a Cole Porter song, was not written until 1953.

A 1940s P.I. with a taste for flashy cars has as his "trademark" a two-tone Edsel. But Edsels rolled off the assembly line in 1957, 1958, and 1959 only. Incidentally, the name "Edsel" quickly became synonymous in American slang with "lemon." Obviously, in this pejorative sense, "Edsel" should be used only in fiction set after 1959.

Editors must be alert to changes in the world around them and the impact such changes have on the language. When "Leningrad" appears on a page, a copyeditor's antennae should go up. The second-largest city in the former Soviet Union was variously known as St. Petersburg (1712–1914), Petrograd (1914–24), and Leningrad (1924–90). In 1991, its residents voted to restore its original name of St. Petersburg—and in doing so, created fertile ground for anachronisms. Which does not mean the copyeditor automatically updates the name to reflect current usage. Instead, she should check the time period covered in the manuscript and make a change only if the usage is incorrect for that period.

Besides signaling the end of the Cold War, the breakup of the Soviet Union has created all kinds of headaches for editors. Reference editors, in particular, now have twelve separate republics to account for, including Russia, which was once used loosely to designate the Soviet Union. In a ripple effect, Czechoslovakia split into the Czech and Slovak Republics, and Yugoslavia ceased to exist as a unified country in 1992, as conflicting ethnic groups waged a civil war.

African countries are another automatic red flag for copyeditors, because many former colonies changed their names on achieving independence. For example, Zambia was once a British protectorate known as Northern Rhodesia. Zimbabwe took that name when it became independent in 1980; it was first known as Southern Rhodesia, a self-governing British colony, later simply Rhodesia, when it unilaterally declared itself a republic. Zaire, a former Belgian colony, used to be known as the Congo and, before that, as the Belgian Congo.

Sometimes the general tone rather than the details is anachronistic. One copyeditor was assigned a young adult novel about the troubled relationship between a teenage boy and his father, a soldier recently returned from the Vietnam War. She found the story compelling, but something about the atmosphere didn't seem right. After a while she put her finger on the problem. The tone of the novel sounded more fifties than early seventies. The kids were too conformist, the setting was tranquil and suburban. When apprised of the problem, the author understood and agreed to fix it. He made a few changes—for example, growing the boy's hair and having his friends smoke pot and his girlfriend run away from home—which were enough to convey the atmosphere of the turbulent Vietnam era.

Perhaps the most common anachronism is the use of outdated slang. (Slang dates very quickly, and good writers use it sparingly and with caution.) "Hippies" didn't exist before the 1960s, so a character in a 1950s book should not be described that way. On the other hand, that was the decade of the "beatniks," so the editor might want to offer that word as a substitute. *But an editor should never presume.* He should merely suggest and leave the decision to the author.

Every generation creates its own slang. "Rad" or "radical" was popular relatively recently; "heavy," "groovy," and "far out" are past examples. All essentially mean "good," but all have had their day. When kids in the late eighties said, "These shoes are bad," or even "She's bad," "bad" paradoxically meant "good." Obviously, "bad" should not be used in that sense by a character in a seventies novel.

Some past expressions, "cool" or "neat," for example, remain current, and some cease to be slang and become part of the common vocabulary. A good ear—and a good memory—will help the editor recognize anachronisms and weed them out.

Historical novels and historical romances are especially vulnerable to anachronisms, particularly when it comes to idiomatic language. It's all too easy to let an occasional "OK" slip in, and some authors might even argue that using such an anachronism is preferable to having accurate historical phrases that sound stilted to the modern ear. But an "OK" in the seventeenth century strikes a jarring note; a middle road is to use neutral language and avoid idioms as much as possible. Most writers of these genres do extensive research and take great pains to get the details correct. But if an author seems careless about historical accuracy, the senior editor will usually alert the copyeditor to this. Occasionally, the copyeditor will be required to do research to sort out which clothes, expressions, and even weaponry go with a particular era. More likely, if the author continues to be careless with the facts, the acquiring editor will decide not to accept future manuscripts.

Logic lapses. A character in a novel takes a "quick look out the window" and proceeds to report on the make and color of several cars she sees. Another character, "glancing into the kitchen," describes every detail, right down to the Cuisinart and the shapes of the wooden knobs on the cabinets.

When you think about it, you realize it's impossible to take in so much at a glance. Furthermore, detailed descriptions of absolutely ordinary scenes add nothing to a book's development. In fact, they risk breaking the flow and, worse, losing the reader. An editor should tactfully alert an author to these problems and possibly suggest cuts.

In another example, an adventure yarn set in "darkest Africa" described an expedition into "cannibal country" taken by the colonial administrator, his young son, twelve British soldiers, and two trackers. Strangely, though, there was no mention of the native bearers who would traditionally carry tents, cots, food, and ammunition, a logic lapse picked up by the copyeditor. Furthermore, when the expedition got to a longhouse in the middle of the jungle, all the soldiers proceeded to get drunk. The copyeditor questioned this with "Would any good colonial type allow his soldiers to get blind drunk in the midst of hostile territory?"

The old caveat *be sure to consider the context* was not heeded by a copyeditor in one case. She reacted with disbelief when, in a teenage romance, she came across an adolescent girl whose "breasts budded and hips curved" at the sight of her first boyfriend. But when the copyeditor queried this with "Give me a break!", she was summarily told by the general editor that the description was "well within the parameters of the genre."

So know your genre. And when in doubt, query with tact. (The copyeditor's query technique in this instance left something to be desired. Humor can sometimes help make a point, but sarcasm has no place on query flags.)

Some genres, such as science fiction and James Bond–type thrillers, have their own internal logic or set of conventions. But logic, or at least the appearance of it, is necessary even in these genres, to carry readers along and persuade them to suspend disbelief.

Readers of these books are ready to go to the most extreme lengths with an author as long as the descriptive details appear to make sense. For example, if a hero is jet-packed into space to stop an incoming enemy missile, there had better be some description (however spurious) of the latest NASA technology that makes this possible (including why his dinner jacket doesn't burn up because of atmospheric friction). It doesn't matter how implausible an action is as long as its "hows and whys" are plausible.

Logic lapses are generally easier to spot in nonfiction than fiction, because the facts can usually be checked. But in technical works, such as a book on computer technology or a manual on nuclear waste, breaks in logic sometimes slip by copyeditors, who tend to be generalists rather than specialists. An editor can often compensate for her lack of "hard" knowledge by watching out for internal inconsistencies, using common sense, and not being shy about querying. But if, despite these efforts, she finds the subject matter beyond her reach, she should say so to her supervisor. Her frankness will be appreciated. It will save potential embarrassment and earn her the respect of her superiors.

Sometimes apparent breaks in logic are actually a result of missing copy. Editors and especially proofreaders should keep an eye out for missing or misplaced pages, as well as dropped paragraphs, sentences, and words.

The Editor's Ear

Editors not only *see* things other readers don't, they also *hear* in a different way. Their editor's "ear" helps them to recognize problems the eye has overlooked. They read aloud to untangle a confusing sentence or clarify an ambiguous phrase. Writers use this trick too, especially to test dialogue for an authentic ring, as well as to try out an alliterative effect or a particular rhythm. They also read out loud for the sheer pleasure of playing with words and experimenting with their sound and placement in a sentence. One senior editor recommended that editors apply their ear in the same way, putting themselves in the writer's shoes.

Editing by ear involves listening for an author's intent (which we will explore later in this chapter under "Common Sense") as well as for the precise meaning of his words. If a sentence has to be read aloud to be understood, the problem may lie in the grammar or the punctuation, or else in the writing itself. So, if a sentence bothers you and you're not sure why, say it aloud and see if it sounds right.

A sentence that needs rereading doesn't necessarily have anything wrong with it. Highly technical matter or theoretical writing or fiction that is particularly dense may require rereading as a matter of course. What we mean here is hitting a snag in a sentence that makes its meaning vague. If such glitches are due to grammar or usage errors, these are easily identified and fixed; if not, the copyeditor should ask the author for clarification rather than guess what was meant.

The following are examples of sentences with grammar or punctuation problems that reading aloud would help pinpoint.

EXAMPLE: "Flying high, she watched the graceful, long-necked geese over the river." Change to: "She watched the graceful, long-necked geese flying high over the river." Dangling modifiers ("flying high") are often easy to miss because the overall sense of a sentence may still be clear to the reader.

EXAMPLE: "When number 24 stopped with the ball he tagged him out." Dangling modifiers can also occur in the middle of a sentence, as "with the ball" does here. "Who tagged whom?" is the question for the author here.

EXAMPLE: "Jane, distraught, promised Saturday night she would see her ex-lover." The reader isn't sure if Jane promised on Saturday to see her ex-lover or promised to see him on Saturday.

EXAMPLE: "This area of Newark has been ravaged by the riot; it doesn't bode well for the future of the neighborhood." *What* doesn't bode well? Again, the sense seems almost clear, but the antecedent of the relative pronoun "it" is not "riot" but the idea the clause expresses. One possible alternative to suggest to the author: "This area of Newark has been ravaged by the riot. The neighborhood's current condition doesn't bode well for its future."

EXAMPLE: "'He's a growing boy,' said Dad, when Sal ordered another slice of pizza with extra cheese and a large Coke." Change to: " . . . another slice of pizza with extra cheese, and a large Coke." Adolescents may be capable of eating anything, but not even Sal would want Coke on his pizza! Adding a comma after "cheese" is all that is needed to resolve the ambiguity.

EXAMPLE: "'Lou,' she pleaded, 'if you have to drink at the bar not at home.'" Change to: "'Lou,' she pleaded, 'if you have to, drink at the bar, not at home.'" Reading this sentence out loud, as dialogue, helps determine where the intended pauses are—and indicates where commas are needed.

EXAMPLE: "When the bus ran off the road, she said the lights went out." Change to: "'When the bus ran off the road,' she said, 'the lights went out.'" The addition of a comma and quotation marks indicates a direct quotation. But the sentence should also be queried because it isn't clear from the context whether "the lights went out" refers to the bus lights or is slang indicating that the speaker momentarily lost consciousness.

Sometimes it's not a sentence but a simple phrase that gives the reader pause, one that, when read aloud, still sounds a little off. Chronic offenders in this category are prepositional phrases.

EXAMPLE: "The ball hit him just down from his knee." Change to: "*below* his knee."

EXAMPLE: "In all the folks up here you won't find another like . . ." Change to: "*among* all the folks."

EXAMPLE: "A red Jag zoomed out behind the police car." Change to: "*from* behind the police car."

If rereading a sentence does not help decipher it, ask yourself this question: *What is the author trying to say?* If you think you know, you can either edit the sentence to make it clearer or suggest alternatives. If you still can't figure it out, simply query. Unclear writing is almost always the result of unclear thinking. It is up to the author—not the editor—to rethink a sentence.

The editor's ear can also detect a false note, particularly in dialogue. Investigating a murder, a sleuth phones a Professor Richard Barnes, an acquaintance of the murdered man but a complete stranger to her. Although he supplies some information, the professor's manner is distant and his tone somewhat patronizing. So when the sleuth hangs up with an airy "'Bye, Rich," the phrase did not ring true to the copyeditor. He queried with "Would she be this casual with a stranger? Change to 'Goodbye, Richard,' or even 'Good-bye, Professor'?" (The author agreed and chose the latter.)

The Editor's Nose

To be a copyeditor, you not only have to have an eye and an ear for the work, you have to have a nose for it as well. One copy chief expressed it this way: "You have to be able to sniff out mistakes, and when you catch their scent, to stay on their trail. Being a copyeditor means being at least part bloodhound."

Suspicion combined with curiosity enables the copyeditor to catch the scent; stubbornness makes her stay on the trail. These are the traits that help a copyeditor smell a rat when one is lurking in the pages of a manuscript.

Being suspicious must become second nature. Just because copy is immaculate, don't assume it's mistake-free. You have to be able to sniff out what's wrong in a sentence or paragraph even when the grammar is correct, the spelling flawless, and the sense clear.

When a mystery writer described a character in his novel as "running along the top of the wall that surrounds Central Park," the copyeditor assigned to the project got what she described as "that nagging feeling." Since she worked in New York, she went out during her lunch hour and found that sure enough, Central Park's low stone wall is not flat on top but actually slopes upward, rendering the action the author described impossible, at least for an ordinary human being.

In another instance, a copyeditor working on a novel set in the Romantic era of the poets Shelley and Keats was stopped short when the hand of an amorous swain began groping its way down a buxom young woman's dress; the logistics seemed off to her. A little research revealed that the tight bodices that were the fashion of the day would have made such shenanigans impossible. The editor even managed to dig up an illustration of a contemporary female fashion plate to prove her point. Now, that's dedication!

Suspicion made another copyeditor visit the Museum of Fine Arts during a trip to Boston to check out the feasibility of a murder committed there by the curator of the Classical collection. It motivated another to go out and buy a six-pack of Red Stripe to see if the Jamaican beer favored by the hard-bitten hero of a modern Western really had a "ruby red" glow.

Of course, copyeditors can get carried away. Freelancers especially should realize that, unless they are specifically requested to do extra research, it will invariably be done on their own time—and at their own expense.

One managing editor was horrified to receive a bill in excess of $2,000 from a freelance copyeditor for editing a modest love story. The editor had taken it upon himself to ride an Amtrak train from New York to Washington and back again to verify the details of the novel, which was set on that particular train. "I did everything the protagonist did," he proudly proclaimed in a cover memo. "Everything" included wining and dining himself, and it was all billed to the publisher.

Our caveat about excessive research also applies to using the telephone, especially in the case of freelancers. As a freelancer, don't call long distance, whether to fact check or to check with an author, unless it's absolutely essential, or authorized. And, as with research, first find out the policy—and get the permission—of the publishing house you're working for. In-house staff should also be circumspect about making long-distance calls.

Following your nose as a copyeditor means using your

WRITING COMMANDMENTS

The following "Writing Commandments" were allegedly copied years ago from a notice in a Capitol Hill committee room. We believe that what's good for writers and the U.S. Congress must certainly be good for editors too.

- Don't use no double negative.
- Make each pronoun agree with their antecedent.
- Join clauses good, like a conjunction should.
- About them sentence fragments.
- When dangling, watch your participles.
- Verbs has to agree with their subjects.
- Just between you and I, case is important too.
- Don't write run-on sentences they are hard to read.
- Don't use commas, which aren't necessary.
- Try to not ever use split infinitives.
- Its important to use your apostrophe's correctly.
- Proofread your writing to see if you any words out.
- Correct spelling is esential.

---

instinct. Often the nose will pick up something both the eye and the ear have missed. When your nose tells you that something's wrong, trust it. To quote one editor, "The nose always knows."

Common Sense

A sense that must be used in conjunction with all the other editing senses is common sense. For an editor, this means understanding a writer's intent and considering his words in context. She does this by listening to what the writer is trying to say and how he is saying it—and never substituting her own voice for his. When an editor alters the subtle meaning of a writer's prose (usually in the name of literal correctness and clarity), the impact is what William Zinsser describes as "one of the bleakest moments for writers . . . when they realize that their editor has missed the point of what they are trying to do."[1]

Take the example of a freelance copyeditor who was assigned a young adult book on censorship, with instructions to do a "light edit." The editor proceeded to excise passages describing how American temperance advocate Carrie Nation had attacked pictures of naked ladies on barroom walls with a hatchet. Her rationale: "You can't mention naked ladies in a book for young people!" Ignoring common sense, the copyeditor had censored not only the content but also the intent of the book.

Another copyeditor carefully deleted all references to dinosaurs in a novel in which they were living contemporaneously with Neanderthals. Strictly speaking, the copyeditor was correct, since dinosaurs disappeared from the Earth long before the advent of our first human ancestors. But the book in question was a sci-fi fantasy, a genre that by definition stretches the bounds of reality. The notion of a young "proto-man" raising a baby dinosaur to be his boon companion is allowable within the parameters of this fictional form.

On the other hand, if an illustration depicting cave dwellers battling an air assault by pterodactyls managed to find its way into a paleontology tome, it should certainly be queried and marked for probable deletion. It should also serve as a warning to the copyeditor to watch for similar anomalies.

Common sense should also be used in editing for sexism. Editing to avoid sexist language and sexist stereotyping—as well as racism and ageism—has become routine, particularly in dealing with children's books, textbooks and other educational materials, and general reference books. Copyediting manuals provide helpful suggestions on how to avoid the generic "he" and how to change sexual stereotypes. "Poetess" becomes "poet," an office boy may turn into an "office worker," the "mailman" becomes a "mail

[1] William Zinsser, *On Writing Well: An Informal Guide to Writing Nonfiction*, 4th. ed. New York: HarperCollins, 1990, p. 270.

125

carrier," and so on. In addition, many publishers have their own guidelines for eliminating sexist language.

Still, copyeditors should use caution in editing a whole book for sexism; a general query to the author or the editor on how to proceed can avoid a lot of problems later. And remember that fiction should almost never be edited to avoid sexism. An author won't thank you for "cleaning up" a character who makes a racial slur, or a man who speaks disparagingly of women; the author most certainly has his or her reasons. Nor should you apply sexism standards to works from the past that you might be summarizing or paraphrasing. Our favorite example of overdoing the correction of "sexist" language appeared in a manuscript that came back from a freelancer with "Peking man" consistently changed to "Peking person."

Using common sense means keeping in mind the type of book you're dealing with and its intended audience when making editing decisions. Keep in mind also the style of the book itself. Sometimes a light touch—not a heavy hand—is required. The sports cliché "staying within oneself" comes to mind. When an athlete says he stays within himself, he means he doesn't do more than he is capable of doing. Similarly, a good editor stays "within" a book and does not do more—or less—than it requires.

Because editors are human, sometimes their senses fail them. When that happens—when you find you've made an error that leaves you red-faced—we suggest you fall back on the one sense that needs no experience or training: your sense of humor. It is that "sixth" sense, to go with memory, eye, ear, nose, and common sense, that every working editor needs to get through a book—and the day.

Knowledge

Knowledge obviously can't be classified as a sense, but we add it here because general knowledge is perhaps more important in editing than in any other profession. Keeping well informed is a process that never ends. As our editor profiles in Chapter 1 indicated, editors keep up to date in many different ways—by reading books and newspapers, magazines and trade periodicals, book reviews and journal articles, by listening to people talk, and by asking questions.

Good editors store their knowledge, clipping and filing articles that may spark an idea for a book. A human-interest news story about how Muslim villagers in the former Yugoslavia welcomed an American family at Christmas by dressing up as characters in the Nativity provided the seed of an idea for a children's book. On the other hand, reading the reviews of two new books on the history of professional baseball's Negro Leagues (and perceiving the market was flooded) dissuaded an editor from accepting a well-written book proposal on the subject.

Editors are always on the lookout for authors as well as for ideas. In scanning book reviews or reading trade periodicals, an editor may come across the name of a writer who would be perfect for a project she has in mind.

Editors also make mental notes of what they have seen and heard—on the news, at a publishing lunch, or even in casual conversation. The tidbits they pick up this way may lead to the discovery of a new writer or cause a last-minute revision to a book in galleys in order to bring it up to date.

For copyeditors in particular, an important (and often overlooked) part of their general knowledge is trivia. All of us accumulate bits and pieces of information just for the fun of it; but editors know that everything they see, hear, learn, or read, however trivial, may come in handy at some time or another.

What proves valuable sometimes surprises even an old hand. In working on a mystery whose characters were killing one another over high-priced "Golden Age" comics, one copyeditor drew on her childhood acquaintance with superheroes to resolve spelling inconsistencies (she knew it was "Aquaman," not "Aqua Man" or "AquaMan"). Another editor used his lifelong love of teas and a knowledge of how to prepare them ("Be sure to warm the pot") when he was assigned a reference book article on the history and culture of tea. And an alert copyeditor's addiction to a TV quiz show saved a publisher embarrassment, possibly even a lawsuit: From the show, she picked up the fact that a fictional U.S. senator depicted as a drunk and a womanizer in a novel she was editing had the same name as a living senator. She alerted the senior editor, who had the author change the character's name. (This example gives credence to the assertion of one copyeditor that "copyeditors have to be the sort of people who win at 'Jeopardy!'")

Sometimes personal experience informs an editor. A guidebook to New York City directed tourists to "take a No. 4 bus up Fifth Avenue to the Bronx" in order to get to The Cloisters, a re-created medieval monastery overlooking the Hudson River. The copyeditor, a New Yorker, happened to know that Fifth Avenue is one-way and the buses go down it, not up, and that The Cloisters is in upper Manhattan, not the Bronx. But any editor should check directions, which can look deceptively correct on the page, especially if they make sense and have no typos.

As we've emphasized all along, a good editor reads omnivorously and is interested in everything. According to one copyeditor, who keeps a "little black book" containing information as diverse as the generic and brand names of drugs and problem spellings such as Art Students (not Students') League, "For the copyeditor especially, knowledge is power, or at least employment."

Special expertise, in addition to general knowledge, can help further an editing career. Until the recent past, the stereotypical book editor was a liberal arts major, perhaps with a graduate degree in English literature. But in this era of specialization, editors now come from many different disciplines. A graduate in psychology might decide to apply her learning to editing psychology textbooks or professional journals. An individual with extensive job experience and contacts in biotechnology may be hired to acquire special projects in that field. An avid sports fan who made her interest known may be regularly assigned books about sports to copyedit and possibly end up as an acquiring editor in that specialty. Choosing a career in editing sometimes allows you to make your avocation your vocation.

Editors can't, of course, know everything. But at the very least they should know how and where to find information when neither a style manual, a copy of *Who's Who*, or a colleague down the hall can come up with a quick answer.

Chapter 5

The Editor's Sensibility

"You must enter into the author's mind, mode, and purpose."

"I think an author's style and vision are extremely important. You sense when something has a creative spark."

"The whole purpose is not to change the author, but to strengthen the book."

(To author:) "This is your book, you are the final arbiter. All I can give you is my passion, my interest, and what I consider my most reasonable judgment."

These statements, all from trade book editors, encapsulate the sensibility a good editor has toward authors and their work. Such a sensibility is not automatic; it develops with a growing knowledge of the craft of editing, through constant reading, and, of course, through the experience of dealing with many kinds of authors and many types of books. In addition, the principles we articulated in Chapter 3—tact, flexibility, confidence, respect for the author, and responsibility to the book—all play a role in developing the editor's sensibility.

Entering into the author's *mind and mode*, understanding the author's *purpose*, implies having literary taste, the ability to recognize good writing; according to one editor, literary taste in turn presupposes being familiar with—and accepting—many different styles of writing as well as having some knowledge of other languages and their literature.

Empathy with a writer's *vision* requires sensitivity to the act of writing and to what the writer goes through in the process of attaining that vision. It entails being able to say to the author, "This is your book" (and meaning it).

Choosing the Books

The editor's sensibility shows itself right at the beginning, with the acquisition process. All editors we talked to agreed that instinct plays a big role in what they choose to buy, whether they're taking on a first novel by an unknown or commissioning an author to write a book on a controversial leader of a religious cult.

"Acquiring books is so subjective," says an editor of historical romances. "We are of course a business, but ultimately editors are readers and go by their gut reaction. I've done some books I didn't think would be very commercial, but that I liked for some reason or other, and some of them turned out well. I'm more and more getting the feel of which books will be a success, but I don't know how to define it."

A mass-market editor agreed that knowing how to buy was a hard quality to define. "There's a lot of talent involved. It's a question of taste and also having a feel for the market."

A trade editor who does mostly quality fiction considers herself lucky because she can begin with what "grabs" her. "Unless my intellect is engaged on a certain level, I won't be a proper editor for the book," she says. Being grabbed is also essential in order for her to "sell" the book to in-house colleagues.

Nonfiction editors, too, rely heavily on instinct as they cast about for original book ideas and try to find the ideal writer to execute each one. These editors are gambling on both the idea and the writer. Will the subject appeal to enough readers to make the book a success? Will a writer who has written a first-class book about a major political scandal in Britain do an equally good job covering a celebrity lawsuit in the United States?

Of course, buying almost any fiction is also something of a gamble (unless it's the work of a sure-fire bestselling author); but fiction editors in most cases have the advantage of basing their decision on a completed manuscript. Nonfiction editors, on the other hand, must rely on a proposal and perhaps a couple of chapters, and on the credentials and track record of the writer. Nonfiction is usually bought this way because the time and cost involved in doing research make it impractical for a writer to submit a completed manuscript; the transaction is always chancy, requiring a leap of faith on the part of the editor. One children's book editor took that leap with an unknown writer, a woman who called her time after time with ideas for books. Said the editor: "She was so persistent, so earnest, and had such a deep desire to write that in the end I responded to her commitment and took a chance on one of her ideas."

An editor who acquires both fiction and nonfiction described the differences as follows: "For nonfiction, you have to find the best person to do the book. For instance, if you want someone to do a birding book, you should choose someone who knows birders. Otherwise the book will languish. You can tell so quickly from a cover letter and two or three pages whether this person is really a professional. In fiction, you have to see the whole novel—the beginning and the end. You can't buy fiction unless you've finished it and loved it." And he added: "I don't think you should ever buy a novel just because you think it will make money, because I've found those are the very books that lose money. It's the ones that stir something inside of you, that create passion, that are ultimately successful."

Obviously, instinct alone is not enough to go on—the demands of the marketplace can never be ignored. But, as the foregoing comments indicate, the decision to buy is in the end a subjective judgment.

The Author/Editor Relationship

Throughout this book we've looked at the author/editor relationship from many angles, examining the role it plays in the acquiring process, in line editing and copyediting, in seeing the manuscript through production, even in sales and promotion. Here we'll focus on how the editor's sensibility can enhance the relationship, improve the quality of the book, and produce psychological benefits for author and editor alike. (This special sensibility is most applicable to trade and mass-market editors, both adult and juvenile. In other areas of publishing, such as textbooks or scholarly books, the author/editor relationship remains important, but the editing tends to be more cut and dried, and content is more crucial than style; in still other areas—reference books such as encyclopedias, dictionaries, and almanacs—where the publisher has ultimate responsibility for the books, author/editor contact may be at a minimum or may not exist at all.)

Getting off to a Good Start

One editor makes it her practice to sit the author down early on in the process and ask him to tell her what his book is about. What is the underlying theme? What does he want to tell readers about his subject if it's nonfiction? If it's fiction, what does he wish to convey through his characters?

"It's helpful to me," she says, "to find out what the author has in mind. Because then I can say, if necessary, 'Well, if you intended to do that, I don't think you've quite succeeded. Your character doesn't quite come through.' Or, 'Your treatment of this aspect of the subject is too skimpy.' Or, in fiction especially, 'Your research is showing. We don't need to know so many facts about the Chesapeake Bay fishing industry.'"

Asking what the book is about sometimes helps focus the

author's thoughts, sometimes clarifies the editor's. It is a way of ensuring early on that author and editor are on the same wavelength.

Negotiating Changes

Most authors are protective of their work, whether it's a finished novel or a carefully worked-out proposal for a non-fiction work. Which is why, as he begins to shape a book, suggesting cuts or additions or even—as sometimes happens in nonfiction—a different approach entirely, an editor needs to establish a relationship of trust with the author. He must not only share the writer's vision, he must also be sensitive to the writer's feelings.

One fiction editor expresses it well: "In dealing with writers, you're dealing with raw, exposed ego, and you have to tread lightly. You must convey to them that you're not there to distort or manipulate their work, but to bring out what they—and you—feel is the best within it."

But sensitivity must be accompanied by honesty. A good editor tells the author honestly what, in her opinion, is good and bad in the manuscript, and about the changes she feels are necessary. But she never forgets that the last word belongs to the author. One editor tells authors to "feel free to edit the editor."

Often, an editor has to persuade an author to cut a book fairly heavily because of the demands of the marketplace; this takes great tact and sensitivity. Nonfiction authors, who generally accumulate an enormous amount of material in the course of their research and are eager to impart it to their readers, may be reluctant to take a lot of it out. It's up to the editor to "make the sale" and convince the author of the need to shorten the book.

Let's look at two different cases in which an author was asked to make heavy cuts. In the first, the editor explained to the author of a teenage mystery that the manuscript had to be cut by a third because of the age of the readers and the demands of the market. But she also convinced the author that the cuts would improve the book rather than diminish it. The pace would be faster, and what the author *knew* about her subject but didn't include would still inform the book and give it weight. In the second example, a book about radio, the preferred length was mentioned by the editor at the outset, but not clearly specified, leaving the author with the feeling that he had a lot of leeway. Only after he'd handed in the entire manuscript was he told that it was much too long and that a hundred pages would have to be cut—preferably by the writer, but if not, by the editor. The reason given was that the greater length would push the book into a higher price bracket and make it more difficult to sell.

The author was shocked by the request at that late stage, and understandably resentful; he reported later that cutting those hundred pages was the hardest part of the whole project. In this instance, the editor showed insufficient sensitivity and also failed to communicate her wishes satisfactorily to the author.

Convincing the author to *add* material also requires sensitivity. By the time a manuscript reaches the editor, the author has lived with it for so long that he or she is usually anxious to get rid of it and in no mood to go back and do further research. Again, the editor needs to make the case, suggesting rather than insisting, persuading the writer that the extra time and work will result in a better (and perhaps more salable) book.

A House Divided

Negotiating changes with one author is not always easy. When two or more authors are involved and they have fundamental disagreements about what course the book should take, it can be a nightmare.

Writers frequently collaborate on a project, each bringing to it different skills and credentials. They almost always start

off with the best of intentions, but since writers have noto-
riously sensitive egos, disagreements—about the writing
style, the approach, the organization, even the method of
working—are apt to occur along the way. We've come across
authors who called the editor constantly to complain about
one another, and authors who had stopped speaking to each
other entirely by the time the manuscript arrived on the
editor's desk. In such cases, the editor may become the court
of last appeal. It will take all her diplomatic skills to be even-
handed, to present herself as the book's advocate, not the
advocate for one or other of the authors.

More often, differences between authors result from different sensibilities. Such a difference arose between the joint
authors of a teenage biography, written in fictionalized form,
about a young woman who headed a spy group and who,
when she was eventually caught and tortured, shot herself
rather than give away her comrades. Her death was described in the first chapter; the rest of the story was told in
flashback. The disagreement arose because one author
wanted to add a second description of the death at the end
of the book in order to emphasize the young woman's hero-
ism, while the other author felt that would be redundant.
Asked to arbitrate, the editor gave her view that the repetition was unnecessary. But rather than laying down the law,
she used all her tact in the course of several long phone
calls and discussions to explain why she felt that a second
death scene would weaken, not strengthen, the impact of
the heroine's martyrdom. The editor showed enough respect
for the objecting author (and for the book) to eventually
convince her.

The Editor as Communicator

As we explained in Chapter 1, once a manuscript is delivered to the publisher, it is the editor's function to keep in
close touch with the author and let her know what to expect—and what will be expected of her.

First-time authors in particular are likely to have only the vaguest notion of what's involved in the process. Educating the author means explaining the various stages of production—edited manuscript, galley proofs, page proofs, and so on—and letting her know who does what and where she fits in. (Some publishers have an "Author's Guide" book or pamphlet for this purpose.)

An unprepared author is likely to be taken aback when her manuscript is returned to her covered with red pencil corrections and with yellow flags flying from page after page. If she'd thought her work was done, she may also be less willing to make suggested changes or answer requests for additional information. And even an experienced author, if she has not published with a particular house before, deserves to be told how the procedures work and what will be expected of her.

The query letter is a useful—and often multipurpose—tool of communication between editor and author. It can be used to explain the general copyediting approach (for example, the manuscript will be marked in red pencil and with colored flags, the spelling and punctuation will generally be according to *Webster's Tenth*, style and usage will follow the *Chicago Manual*), to ask the author to supply more information, or to clarify specific issues in the manuscript. It may also give the author information about the schedule.

Figure 5.1 is a query letter to the author of a feature article on Venice slated to appear in an encyclopedia yearbook. Note the courteous tone of the letter and the tact with which the editor questions certain statements and asks for more information. Note also his expressed appreciation of the article and for the author's promptness in submitting it. As long as it is not overdone, a little flattery goes a long way, and writers are no exception to that rule.

The sensitive editor also keeps communication lines open with other staff members; for example, she gives the copyeditor whatever information she needs to do a particular job well, and she works closely with production people

Dear Professor Montale:

Many thanks for sending us your article on Venice so promptly. The level seems just right for our readership, and the article makes very entertaining as well as informative reading.

After the piece is edited, I will send a copy of the manuscript for your review, along with any queries that arise in the course of editing. Before editing gets underway, however, we would much appreciate your responding to the following questions:

> Page 3, 2nd full para.: Could you add a few words on the battle of Lepanto here? Isn't it famous enough (e.g., as the subject of important paintings) to warrant a mention?

> Page 4, top: After the grand tour description, could you add a paragraph on some of the great writers, artists, and musicians who drew on Venice for inspiration? This would fit nicely with your later statement that "Venice belongs to us all."

> Page 8, second para.: Could you add a few words on recent developments, for example, such subjects as the projected subway connection from Venice to the mainland and Lido, and the Italian Parliament's approval of a financing scheme for lagoon cleanup and sea defenses.

> Page 8, final para.: What is this "international conservation project"? Is it the UNESCO campaign mentioned on page 6?

> Page 17, lines 2-5: When were the horses removed from the basilica entrance? Were they replaced? Were replicas put outside? (Photographs from the 1980s seem to show them in position.)

Could you supply a short bibliography listing some of the main general sources on Venice's history and culture (in addition to your own book) and perhaps on efforts to preserve the city? This would appear at the end of the article.

Again, thank you very much for your article and for your attention to these points.

Sincerely,

Leonard English

Leonard English
Senior Editor

Figure 5.1

so schedules can be met. She also maintains contacts with her favorite agents, keeping them up to date on the progress of books they have sold to her or authors they have recommended, and letting them know what she's looking for in the way of future projects.

Courtesy Counts

Keeping others informed is also a matter of simple courtesy. Authors appreciate being told when edited manuscript or page proofs are scheduled to arrive and how much time they will have to work on them. Most authors want to do the best possible job for their book; when they are given the schedule in advance, many will adjust their own schedules so as to be available to read manuscript or proofs.

Courtesy includes being *accessible*—to authors, agents, and colleagues. The courteous editor responds promptly to agents' submissions and returns their phone calls within a reasonable time. He is also accessible to his authors, who may be struggling with their work or may simply need a sympathetic listener.

"Authors are grateful and gracious," says one children's book editor. "Writing is a lonely job and sometimes they just need to talk and get some reassurance." A mass-market editor of women's fiction agrees. "I make it a point to be accessible," she says. "I hate it when I hear a writer say, 'I'm afraid to call my editor' or 'I'm afraid to call my agent.' The answer is, Get a new editor or a new agent."

The smart editor is also responsive to the concerns of colleagues in other departments. For example, if the editor learns that an author will be late returning proofs, he passes that information along to production; if the publicity department asks for biographical material on one of his authors, he fulfills the request at the earliest opportunity. Being courteous helps others do their job better; it also makes the working day more pleasant.

Telling It Like It Is

If an editor is to win his authors' trust, he must be honest with them. And not just about the work itself, but about the realities of the marketplace. Authors, especially new ones, tend to have unrealistic expectations for their book, and especially about what the publisher will do to promote it. The harsh reality is that few books, even the most worthy ones, get more than a tiny slice of the sales and promotion pie (most of it being eaten up by bestsellers or projected bestsellers), and the vast majority make only the briefest appearance on bookstore shelves, thereafter to disappear forever. It is the thankless but worthwhile task of the senior editor to give authors a crash course in what the business is. Doing so may at least alleviate authors' disappointment, and perhaps reduce feelings of resentment, which will inevitably be directed toward the editor.

One trade editor makes it her business to present writers with the worst-case scenario. "I can cite so many examples of works of great literary merit, even by established writers, that have never sold, or never gotten picked up by the reviewers. I explain that your publicist is going to do only so much, that we will probably not advertise the book unless it starts taking off. I explain to them the difference between my enthusiasm and the enthusiasm they're likely to get from the house."

While preparing her authors for "failure," at least in the commercial sense, this editor is conveying to them that she herself supports them and believes in their talent.

A Professional Friend

Most senior editors feel strongly about their authors. At different times they feel protective, supportive, affectionate, responsible, impatient, exasperated, or frustrated. But almost without exception, they *care*.

For one children's book editor, working directly with authors is the most rewarding part of the job. She sees herself as an adviser and friend to her authors, and her hope is to help develop a writer's whole career, not just work on a single book. Some editors think of their authors as their friends and may have a social as well as a professional relationship with them. Others stress the importance of keeping the relationship within professional bounds. "It's as simple," a fiction editor said, "as the fact that your writers can leave you at any time. Some writers are very loyal to their editors despite the fact that a better offer may come along. Others will go to the highest bidder. But it hurts to lose an author when you've poured your heart and soul into her work, especially if you've begun to feel (and this is the danger of getting too close) that you're partially responsible for her success."

Too much identification with authors can also be detrimental to an editor's career. Editors cannot afford to forget that they have a responsibility to the publisher—their employer—as well as to the author. They cannot allow themselves to become the author's advocate at the expense of the house. When an author makes unreasonable demands—wanting final say over the cover design, for example, or insisting on making heavy and unwarranted changes in proofs at the last minute—the editor must weigh the interests of the house against those of the author. It is the editor, after all, who will ultimately be held responsible for the book's success or failure in the marketplace.

Learning to Think Like a Writer

In *The Art of Fiction*, John Gardner debunks the popular notion that writers are born, not made. "Though the ability to write well is partly a gift," he says, "writing ability is mainly a product of good teaching supported by a deep-down love of writing."[1] He also stresses the necessity of practice for the writer, and the importance of education:

> No one can hope to write really well if he has not learned how to analyze fiction—how to recognize a symbol when it jumps out at him, how to make out theme in a literary work, how to account for a writer's selection and organization of fictional details.[2]

Being able to edit well, like being able to write well, may be a talent. But it is also a skill. The editor's instinct—knowing how, when, and to what degree to intervene in a text—is developed and honed through practice.

Practice, for both editors and writers, starts with reading. Writers read to learn how other writers work, how they use literary devices and achieve stylistic effects. They are craftspeople appraising another's work, admiring—or critiquing—not only the finished product but also its individual parts.

Editors, too, read in a particular way. Whereas the average reader finishes a book and pronounces it good or bad, the editor goes further, asking why it succeeded or failed, studying its structure and style, considering how it could be improved.

Practice helps sharpen an editor's craft; empathy deepens it. Too often, writers complain that editors don't understand what they are getting at and hence make insensitive changes (or suggestions) that do violence to that writer's work. This is why it is important for an editor to learn how to think like a writer, which means understanding at least the basics of the writing process.

Gardner suggests writers should "go to school" to learn how to write. We believe editors should study *how* writers write. Much is made of the need for writers to know craft, from the rudiments of constructing a sentence to the intricacies of composing a poem; there are almost as many books sold and courses offered on the subject as there are aspiring

---

[1] John Gardner, *The Art of Fiction*. New York: Random House, 1991, p. ix.
[2] Ibid., p. 13.

writers. Yet few, if any, of these books are geared specifically to instructing editors about the process of writing, about the components that go into building a story or even a single sentence.

In our view, the best way for editors to learn about writing is from writers themselves. Editors need to listen to writers talk—about their work, about themselves, and about the creative process.

In *The Art of Fiction*, John Gardner cogently breaks down fiction into its various components—plot, character, sentence structure, diction—and shows how they are assembled to make a novel. Though William Zinsser's *On Writing Well*[3] is billed as an "informal guide to writing nonfiction," its lively advice is applicable to fiction as well. In *The Writing Life*,[4] Annie Dillard offers a sensitive glimpse into the writing process, which will help editors empathize with the writer at work. John Braine's *Writing a Novel*[5] offers aspiring writers (and interested editors) a conducted tour of his workshop, introducing the tools of fiction writing and demonstrating their use with examples from his own work and that of many distinguished writers. And editors and writers alike should sleep with *The Elements of Style*[6] under their pillows. This slim volume, a classic, argues the "case for cleanliness, accuracy, and brevity in the use of English" and contains a section on style that is a model of literary sense and sensibility. These books have the rare and delightful virtue of practicing what they preach: They are all very well written.

In the next section, we review some key elements of strong writing as well as some common pitfalls. Our aim is to make it easier for editors to pinpoint problems in a manuscript and give them the tools to come up with appropriate solutions.

---

[3] William Zinsser, *On Writing Well: An Informal Guide to Writing Nonfiction*, 4th ed. New York: HarperCollins, 1990.
[4] Annie Dillard, *The Writing Life*. New York: HarperCollins, 1990.
[5] John Braine, *Writing a Novel*. New York: McGraw-Hill, 1975.
[6] William Strunk Jr. and E. B. White, *The Elements of Style*, 3rd ed., with index. New York: Macmillan, 1979.

Some Elements of Good Writing

Showing, Not Telling

Anyone interested in writing has come across the maxim "Show, don't tell." Yet experienced writers as well as beginners often make the mistake of telling too much. Excessive telling essentially means too much description; the result is inanimate, tedious prose. Compare the following two sentences:

"Eddie, a Vietnam vet, was living on the streets."

"Eddie squatted on his haunches like a Vietnamese peasant, against the backdrop of a gracious old townhouse, and gnawed on a hunk of stale bread."

The second sentence, in context, had far more impact than a simple statement of fact. Creative writers "show" their readers whatever subjective truth they wish to convey, in part by painting a word picture of events instead of merely iterating them.

A giveaway sign of too much telling is that you, the reader, start getting bored and begin skipping paragraphs, even pages. More than likely you are becoming bogged down in overly long narrative. As an editor, you have to be able to identify when narrative works and when it could—and should—be replaced by more direct showing modes such as anecdote, action, or dialogue.

For example, in a story whose theme was racism, an author described her "country cousin" as being afraid as they drove through an inner-city neighborhood. The editor asked the author to portray rather than just allude to her cousin's fear. In a revised version of the story, the author showed her cousin, who was driving the car, running a red light and risking both women's lives so as not to be "trapped" at an intersection. Ironically, they themselves were then stopped by the police—two black officers. Here, showing not only made the writing more vivid, it also added resonance to the story's theme.

Removing Scaffolding and Building Bridges

"Remove all scaffolding!" a renowned fiction editor used to exhort his authors. What he meant was that the way the work has been constructed, its preliminary stages, should never be apparent. Scaffolding usually takes the form of needless explanation—in other words, overwriting.

Overwriting afflicts both fiction and nonfiction. In nonfiction it tends to take the form of repetitions that hammer home a point ad nauseam and become a sort of *re*-recapitulating. In a psychological case study, a woman's mother died when she was very young—a key trauma, according to the author, which he referred to at virtually every mention of the subject's chronic depression. The editor deleted some references outright and suggested others for deletion.

Authors often overtell because they want to make sure that the reader gets what they are trying to say. One of the most helpful—and most liberating—bits of advice an editor can give a writer is to trust the reader. He or she *will* get the point, without being hit over the head with it.

At times, writers underwrite rather than overwrite. Underwriting is fairly easy to spot. The reader finds himself saying, "Something's missing here." What's missing may be a descriptive detail, a tidbit of information, or a link in the logical progression of a piece; it stops the flow of the writing and gives the reader pause. What the author needs to do in this case is "build a bridge," supplying the missing word, sentence, or transitional paragraph. Writers generally underwrite because they know their material so well that they assume the reader knows it too. It is up to the editor to remind them to put those vital connections down on the page.

Figure 5.2 is an example of an edited manuscript page—in fact, it's from the section you just read, with some extra mistakes thrown in.

Removing Scaffolding and building Bridges

~~One way of thinking of telling is as "scaffolding."~~ "Remove all scaffolding"! a renowned fiction editor used to exhort his authors. What he meant was that the [way the work has been constructed, its preliminary stages,] ~~artistry behind a work~~ should never be apparent. "Scaffolding," ~~the articulation of the writers creative process~~ usually takes the form of needless explanation[. in other words, overwriting.]

~~Excessive telling, and~~ overwriting ~~in general~~ afflicts both fiction and nonfiction. In nonfiction[, it] ~~especially, overwriting~~ tends to take the form of repetitions that hammer home a[n] ~~important~~ point ad nauseam, and become a sort of rerecapitulating. ~~For instance~~ in a psychological case study, a woman's mother died when she was very young--a key trauma, according to the author[, which he referred to] ~~This point the author seemed to insert~~ at virtually every mention of the subject's chronic depression. ~~some of these~~ [Some references] the editor deleted outright[;] ~~others she~~ suggested [and others] for deletion. Authors often overtell because they ~~are anxious~~ [want to make sure] that the reader gets what they ~~are~~ trying to say. One of the most helpful--and most liberating--bits of advice an editor can give a writer is to trust the reader. He or she will get the point, without being hit over the head with it.

~~Just as~~ [At times,] writers over write ~~they also~~ under-write[, rather than.] Underwriting is fairly easy to spot. The reader finds himself saying, "Something's missing here." What's missing may be a descriptive detail, a tidbit of information, or a link in the logical progression of a piece; it stops the flow of the writing and gives the reader pause. What the author needs to do in this case is "build a bridge," supplying the missing ~~phrase~~ [word,] sentence, or transitional paragraph. ~~The usual reason that~~ writers [generally] underwrite ~~is that~~ [because] they know their material so well ~~they neglect to verbalize it in writing: they seem to~~ [that they] assume ~~that~~ the reader knows it too. ~~Even the most experienced authors sometimes underwrite, and~~ [It] is up to the editor to remind them to put those vital connections down on the page.

Figure 5.2

Being Concrete

Virtually the first thing a writer learns is don't generalize, be specific. Don't say that a man is wearing a hat; tell us whether it's a fedora or a baseball cap, whether it's brown or red, battered or brand-new. Don't tell us that a woman is nasty; show her berating the mail carrier or gossiping maliciously about a neighbor. Don't state that it's a perfect spring day; make us feel the soft breeze and smell the flowers and fresh-turned earth. The first question an editor should ask about descriptive writing is: Does the description evoke a concrete image? Can readers *see* what a writer is trying to show them?

The second test of imagery is more subtle. The editor must ask: Are the details significant as well as vivid? Significant details do more than create a strong word picture. They communicate the essence of a person, place, or experience or enhance the author's plot or thematic purpose. Insignificant or irrelevant details merely bog down the prose.

A story described Emily "walking off in the wake of her huge German shepherd," conjuring up a clear and amusing image. But the description also heightened the story's theme, which was how people construct myths to reassure themselves that they are safe. Speaking about a neighbor who was recently murdered, Emily had just insisted to a friend, "If that guy'd had a dog, he'd still be alive." Emily's myth of safety was having a huge German shepherd.

In another story, Jack O'Hanlon is an elderly man struggling to live with dignity in the city. He says of himself, "I was a hellion, I was. Two hundred and fifty pounds of solid mahogany." Jack, "who drove horses before a truck," now "cooks and cleans for himself and once a month takes down his curtains to wash and iron them." These details individualize Jack and make him real to the reader. They also make him more human, and therefore more sympathetic. The juxtaposition of the images shows that Jack was young once and that his present concerns will be ours as we age. Getting readers to see Jack as like themselves is the first step to having them feel compassion for him—and for elderly people in general.

Using "Strong" Language

Verbs. Verbs are the engine of a sentence; they supply the power and move it ahead. They set the pace and tone of a sentence and provide nuance and color. "Look at how an author uses verbs," an editor told us, "to see how well he writes."

Current literary fashion dictates that short words in general, and especially short verbs, are better than long words. Likewise, the active has superseded the passive voice. Short, active verbs do convey more punch and immediacy. New writers especially are advised to use them, since beginners tend to mistake florid prose for beautiful language. But, as the previous sentence shows, there is a place for the passive. An editor should never ban a construction from a writer's repertoire but rather evaluate each one in context. Moreover, too much of anything becomes boring; varying constructions, as well as the length of words and sentences, and using different rhythms make for a lively writing style.

Good writing is economical but not necessarily comprised of only short sentences and short words. Economy means that every word should count and make a contribution to the writer's purpose.

The sentence "The sound of the fire siren outside my window woke me up" (the first line of a new chapter) conveys information. But change it to "The fire siren dying directly below my window startles me from sleep" and you set a scene and communicate urgency. The difference is in the verbs. The phrase "the fire siren dying" allows us to hear its wail; "startles me from sleep" evokes the sense of a sudden, rude awakening. These verbs put us in the center of the action and make us want to read on, which is the author's purpose.

In the same chapter, the protagonist, fearing what turns out to be a false alarm, "corrals" her "cranky old feline in her carrier." "Corrals" is not only more vivid than, say, "puts" would be, but its unusual use—in this context—turns an ordinary word into a whimsical image. Later, after banishing a mouse from the kitchen, the cat "blinks up" at her mistress, "then saunters off, a spring in her arthritic step." If the cat had merely "looked up" and "walked away," the effect would have been less vivid and also less true. As cat lovers know, cats tend to be nonchalant in triumph.

But even strong, descriptive verbs should not be used in excess. "Walk" may be the right word as opposed to "saunter," "amble," or "stroll," when the walking itself is peripheral to the action being described. And "said" is often better than "remark," "utter," or "declare," words that often have the effect of cluttering dialogue and distracting attention from what the character is saying.

Adjectives. When it comes to adjectives, less is definitely more. Writer-publisher Sol Stein calls this principle the "one plus one equals one-half" rule:

> It means that if two adjectives are used, either one will probably produce a stronger effect than the two together; if two phrases say the same thing in different ways, the effect will be strengthened by choosing the better of the two and dropping the other. . . . The same principle applies to works as a whole: ten strong scenes are better than ten strong scenes plus two weaker scenes.[7]

Writers, especially beginners, often overuse adjectives. They want to be precise, to communicate accurately the details of what they are trying to describe. But a good writer, like a painter, strives to capture an object's essence, the one characteristic that will fix it in the reader's mind. Too many adjectives, as opposed to a single telling one, blur the picture and divert the reader's attention.

[7] Gerald Gross, ed., *Editors on Editing*. New York: Harper & Row, 1985, p. 57.

Take the phrase "a tall, yellow-faced, sleepy sunflower." "Sleepy" is the essential quality the author wants to portray; it offers the image of the sunflower nodding in the sun. "Yellow-faced" isn't, since everyone knows sunflowers are yellow. The phrase "a tall, languorous sunflower" creates that image in leaner, more focused language.

The damselfly and green darner are two species of dragonfly. A writer described them in a sentence as "the elegant damselfly and sturdier green darner." The juxtaposition of "elegant" and "sturdy" effectively conveys the difference between the two species. ("Elegant" also complements the "damsel" in damselfly.) Later, she described them both as "my skittish escorts as I walk along the river." In a single word, "skittish," she captured the most familiar characteristic of dragonflies—their quick, darting motion—and also their shyness.

A profitable and pleasurable way for writers and editors alike to learn how to use adjectives is to read poetry. Poets are ever in search of the clear, concrete image, which they primarily achieve through the sparing use of adjectives. Take, for instance, "In a Station of the Metro," a *haiku* like poem by Ezra Pound:

> *The apparition of these faces in the crowd;*
> *Petals on a wet, black bough.*[8]

What could be simpler, or more striking, than the image "petals on a wet, black bough"? Its strength derives from the contrast in colors (we presume the petals are pale) and textures (the soft petals on the rough branch). The image is the more evocative because it is largely implicit: Pound truly shows, not tells.

Adverbs and qualifiers. Adverbs have a specific job to do— to modify other words, especially verbs, and thus to enhance their meaning.

---

[8] Ezra Pound, *Selected Poems of Ezra Pound*. New York: New Directions, 1957, p. 35.

For example, if an old woman "laughed loudly in church" or a young lover "smiled wistfully at the news," we know more precisely what that character did or felt than if she or he had just "laughed" or "smiled." It's when a bum "shambles awkwardly" or a wolf "growls menacingly" that adverbs lose their force. "Awkwardly" is implied in "shambled," as is "menacingly" in "growled." When they reiterate the inherent meaning of verbs, adverbs weaken them.

Fiction editors keep an eye out for needless adverbs in dialogue. In an effort to convey a character's mood, writers will say things like "'No,' he snapped tersely," or "'Yes,' she sighed softly." But if a character has been well drawn, how he or she says something will be clear from the context, and phrases like "he laughed maniacally" and "she whispered icily" are superfluous.

In addition to "lazy" adjectives and "overkill" adverbs, high on editors' hit lists are little qualifying words: "sort of," "kind of," "a little," "a bit," "quite," "rather," "very," and so on. These words slip "rather" easily into writing because they are used so frequently in conversation. But by qualifying a description, they generally weaken it. Being "sort of mad" is like being "a little pregnant." If you're mad, you're mad, and if you're not that angry, "irritated" is a better word to describe your feelings.

Too many little qualifiers have the effect of making writing sound tentative. And a writer whose language is a little tentative seems rather unsure of his subject and kind of unprofessional.

Avoiding Weak Language

Pet words and phrases. A common writing "sin," committed by both fiction and nonfiction writers, is the overuse of pet words and phrases. Writers tend to overuse words that they favor in their own speech; or else they fall in love with a phrase and fail to notice that it's popping up in every paragraph and that, as a result, its impact is considerably lessened.

One nonfiction writer seemed driven to punctuate every point with "as it were." Others favored "ergo" (from the Latin for "therefore, hence"), "at any rate," "the bottom line is," and "at the end of the day."

One novelist became enamored of the phrase "arms akimbo." Her characters always seemed to stand "with arms akimbo" when expressing strong emotion. Aside from the fact that people don't have to stand with their hands on their hips to show their feelings, "arms akimbo" is a somewhat archaic phrase that should be used conservatively—in this case, perhaps as a mannerism exhibited by a character in a particular mood.

It is the editor's job to decide how much is too much and to limit the use of pet words and phrases accordingly. Writers are often amazed to discover how often they've used a particular expression. Even so, they are often attached to their "pets," and editors should show tact in excising them.

The echo effect.   Writers sometimes have a tendency to repeat words—especially adjectives and verbs—in consecutive sentences, or even in the same sentence. Sometimes this happens because a word just used is still echoing in the writer's head.

For instance, "It was an *immaculate* new building. . . . His hair was *immaculately* combed." Or: "She *raced* down the street, *racing* around the corner to meet him." An editor can suggest, but shouldn't arbitrarily substitute another word. A query such as "Note repetition 'immaculate'/'immaculately' here; another adjective/adverb possible for variety?" is sufficient.

Another common form of repetition is beginning successive sentences with the same phrase, such as "There are," "There is," or "It is." The editor should put check marks in the margin next to the repeats and a query to the effect, "Note repetition 'There are'; possible to vary one?" or "OK to vary as indicated?"

Sometimes editors come across a whole sentence or even a paragraph that they think has appeared in its exact form previously. (This is where the editor's memory is invaluable.) If this happens, you should try to track down the repetition and at least flag it for the author's attention. Repetitions of any kind quickly bore readers, even if they're not completely conscious of them. Good writing is never static or unvaried.

You may ask why an author wouldn't notice such repetitions, especially in obvious cases such as these. But it's very easy to overlook flaws in your own writing, largely because you're too close to it. (Which is why authors shouldn't be the only ones to proofread their work, and, ideally, copyeditors shouldn't proof the galleys of a manuscript they have edited.)

Metaphors and similes. Metaphors and similes are important components of strong writing. When a thing is said to be *like* something else, this is a simile; things that *are* something, symbolically, are metaphors. When they work, metaphors and similes give writing resonance. What concerns us here is when—and why—they don't work.

Metaphors and similes shouldn't be used just for the sake of using them. If something can be stated in straightforward prose, especially if it's factual information, then that's how it should be presented. In the sentence "The germ for W's article was born on the date when his temperature was raised by an editorial," the metaphors fail because they are strained. A good metaphor doesn't jump off the page; it leads the reader back into the writing. The editor discreetly suggested that this sentence be changed to: "The inspiration for W's article was an editorial."

Mixed metaphors are weak metaphors. For instance, "His political ascendance was gathering speed." What this author probably meant to say was "His political star was on the ascent." This version solves the problem of the mixed metaphor; but it introduces another problem, namely the clichéd metaphor. An author who wrote "The settlers scattered to the four winds on the wings of fear" was persuaded by her editor to change that bit of purple prose to "The settlers scattered across the countryside in fear for their lives."

Like weak metaphors, weak similes are usually clichéd or strained. Clichéd similes abound in every kind of writing: "high as a kite," "pure as the driven snow," "happy as a clam." Clichés become clichés because they are truisms that have been repeated endlessly. Clichéd similes should be avoided because they have become so stale that they no longer evoke any image at all. Platitudes such as "Procrastination is the thief of time," "This too shall pass," and "No pain, no gain" fall into the same category.

Compare the above clichés with the description of a skinflint: "as tight as the bark on a tree." This simile works because it evokes a fresh image: the idea of bark clinging to a tree as tightly as a miser clings to his cash. But since it has a rural, homespun feel, the simile would probably not work if it were applied to a stingy Wall Street stockbroker. Both similes and metaphors should be appropriate to the context in which they are used.

Among the best similes are those that work visually. One novelist described a gossipy character, Mary, as having "ears like a lynx." What makes the simile vivid—and fun—is that it conjures up the image of a woman with ears that are tufted like a lynx's as well as upright and attentive. The simile also works in context because Mary has more than once been referred to as "catty."

An example of a strained simile is "like a concert pianist hurrying to catch up with the symphony." The author meant to convey the image of a man who had fallen behind in a race and was desperate to make up the distance between him and others. The problem is twofold: First, the image itself is a reach and second, it doesn't make sense. A musician cannot play faster to catch up—if he fell behind, he would just jump to where the orchestra was in the score.

If a writer forces an image, chances are the image itself will be forced. Metaphors and similes that come naturally usually sound natural.

Dialogue

"I've written the most wonderful play," the young playwright exclaimed. "I went away for the weekend and taped the house guests' conversation. It's called *Weekend in the Country*."

Needless to say, this play was never produced. Dialogue is not the literal rendering of what people say but the extraction of the essence of their speech, shaped to reflect the writer's intent. Dialogue is the ultimate "showing" because everything—characterization, ideas, and even some off-stage action—is communicated through spoken language.

But since dialogue must sound realistic—capturing the rhythm of how people talk as well as the turns of phrase that mark their words as their own—it has a certain leeway.

For example, the little qualifiers referred to previously are acceptable in dialogue, as are clichés and platitudes when they are used as signature words to help draw a character. How people speak is really a voiceprint of who they are; it can tell us where they're from, their class and cultural background, and their level of education. For this reason, certain ungrammatical usages (e.g., "I ain't" or "he don't") and occasional incorrect spellings (e.g., "nuthin'" for "nothing") are also permissible in dialogue.

Inexperienced fiction writers seem to begin nearly every sentence of dialogue with interjections such as "well," "umm," "huh," "oh," or "ah." In their attempt to replicate speech, they are overburdening it with words that, when actually spoken, usually aren't heard. The listener tends to tune them out and go right to the speaker's message.

In good writing, such devices are used sparingly, even in dialogue. The effect of using too many qualifiers—for instance, to show a character as tentative—will be to annoy the reader.

As Aristotle wrote in the *Poetics*, art is an imitation of life. Dialogue is not speech, it imitates it, just as fiction does not replicate life, it mirrors it. "But she really sounds like that," the new writer may protest. Perhaps the editor's best response is to remind the writer that just because something happened in life does not necessarily mean that it makes a believable or compelling story. Any writer of serious fiction has to discriminate between what is fact and what is true. Fact is the "truth" of investigative reporters and journalists; what is "true" is not a literal rendering of the facts but the truth as the creative writer sees it and seeks to convey it to the reader.

A final caveat: Thinking like a writer helps you recognize writing problems and get a sense of how they can be corrected. It does *not* mean that you, the editor, should usurp the writer's role. As we've emphasized throughout this book, the editor's role is to refine, suggest, and advise. Developing an editor's sensibility will enable you to fulfill that role in a way that will satisfy the writer—and you. And that is no mean feat.

Chapter 6

A Guide to Editorial Freelancing

The book business offers a wealth of opportunities for anyone contemplating freelancing. Today's publishers farm out freelance work at virtually every stage of a book's life, beginning with the early development and shaping of the manuscript and continuing through design, editing and production, and the preparation of the index.

The "Big Three"

Freelancing's "big three"—and our main focus here—are editing, proofreading, and indexing. This is where most of the work is. All trade divisions (adult and juvenile fiction and nonfiction) use freelance copyeditors and proofreaders, as do reference publishers, textbook publishers (both college and el-hi), publishers of professional books (e.g., medical and legal books), and university presses.

Freelance editing primarily means copyediting, especially when it's for trade book houses. But like their in-house counterparts, freelance copyeditors are increasingly responsible for more than just style, grammar, and usage and some basic fact checking. A freelance assignment billed as "copyediting" may also require some line editing and even rewriting. Substantive and developmental editing are more likely to come from nontrade sources such as textbook and professional book publishers. And for freelancers who are computer literate, an editing project may include editing on screen a manuscript that was submitted on disk, electronically coding a manuscript for the typesetter, and/or electronically inserting corrections made by an in-house editor.

Proofreading is generally available from the sources that farm out copyediting (and there's usually more of it).

Indexing, perhaps more than any other editorial function, is the province of freelancers; most publishers don't have indexers on staff, and many if not most nonfiction books, from biographies to encyclopedias, require indexes. Which implies that if you develop a taste for indexing—and the competence to do it well—chances are you'll find work. But indexing *is* a special taste. According to Carol O'Neill and Avima Ruder, "Indexing is like eggplant: Freelancers either hate it or love it."[1]

Since indexes have not been dealt with elsewhere in this book, a brief description is in order here. An index is an alphabetical listing of the persons and places, facts and concepts in a text, followed by the numbers of the pages on which they appear. Its purpose is to help the reader find what he or she is looking for as quickly and easily as possible.

Typically, there are three stages to preparing an index. In the first read, the indexer goes quickly through the pages to get an overall sense of what concepts, names, and so on are important enough to be indexed. The second read is more deliberate, allowing the indexer to circle or underline pertinent words and phrases, usually in colored pencil. In the third read, the indexer checks his or her work and writes each individual entry on an index card—or, more commonly now, inputs the entries into a computer with an indexing program that will sort them alphabetically. If working by hand, the indexer then alphabetizes the cards, edits them, and finally types the index in the style that conforms to the publisher's specifications.

Indexing is more complex than the above description in-

[1] Carol L. O'Neill and Avima Ruder, *The Complete Guide to Editorial Freelancing*. New York: Harper & Row, 1979, p. 128.

dicates. Distinguishing important concepts—especially concepts that are not clearly defined—requires great skill; and even names, particularly foreign ones, may pose problems. The indexer also has to decide which entries should be subdivided and how many subentries to make, and he must know when and how to cross-reference entries.

"An indexer has to be able to work slowly and methodically," says a freelance veteran. "Patience, along with attention to detail, is the key to success." Indexers must be able to stay patient under pressure, since their work is the last phase of book preparation and is invariably a rush job. They must have a broad enough general knowledge to make judgments about what is important—and what is not—in a specific text, as well as the editorial know-how to edit and style their completed work. "It's a little like having a split personality," says another indexer. "You have to be totally compulsive and concerned with details, yet able to see the big picture too."

How do you learn how to index? Beginners might start by reading the indexing sections included in editing style manuals and go on to some more detailed works on the subject (see "Annotated Bibliography," Chapter 8). Reading some representative indexes can be helpful, and so can proofreading a few. Proofing and checking indexes (which consists primarily of ascertaining that entries are spelled correctly and styled consistently and are to be found on the page the indexer has indicated) give one a sense of how much work goes into an index as well as of the particular problems that must be resolved when preparing one.

Who Freelances and Why?

There are as many editorial freelancers as there are reasons to freelance. Some freelance full-time, some part-time. Some freelance as a career, others to support another career, often in the arts. Some freelance after they've worked in-house; some decide to leave in-house work to freelance. Some alternate between the two, depending on where they are in their career or their personal life; others work in-house and freelance simultaneously. Some are forced to freelance because they've been laid off from their in-house jobs. Others with no editorial experience learn freelance skills as a new career. And still others turn to freelancing as a way of earning additional income in their retirement years. (It's also worth noting that freelancing does not necessarily imply working out of house; there are lots of in-house freelancers.)

The skill levels of freelancers vary widely. One may be an experienced out-of-work senior editor trying to stay visible by doing manuscript evaluation and substantive editing until an appropriate in-house position opens up. Another may be a musician with little interest in a publishing career who picks up an occasional proofreading job to make some quick extra cash. For some, freelancing offers an opportunity to advance other areas of their careers. Writers who work as freelance editors can keep up with what's going on in the book business and often make valuable in-house contacts who may be prospects to publish their writing.

Good freelancers—particularly those who demonstrate that they have other skills, such as the ability to organize their work and to relate well to other people—often succeed in using their experience as a springboard to in-house work. Both authors of this book have worked in-house and as freelancers; both found freelancing attractive because it afforded them more time to write. As a result of freelancing, both were offered in-house jobs, one as a project director on a nature guide, the other as a senior editor in a reference department.

Pros and Cons of Freelancing

"It spoils you—you get to love being your own boss." That's how a successful medical editor summed up what's best about the freelance life.

As her own boss, a freelancer is free to set her own hours.

It's no accident that many freelancers are night owls who don't function well in the morning. And flexible hours allow part-time freelancers to arrange work around personal responsibilities or even in conjunction with another job.

Independent types, freelancers treasure their ability to pick and choose their projects, to say "no" to something, which they couldn't do in-house. Of course, saying "no" to a publisher more than once in a while is risky. Unless freelancers are very good and well established, the jobs may stop coming their way.

Because they generally work at home, freelancers don't have to cope with commuting, office politics, or even other people. As one of them put it: "I don't want to have to pay attention to the pecking order. When I work, I want to work, and there are too many distractions in-house."

Finally, freelancers enjoy certain tax benefits. They can deduct part of their rent or mortgage payments, as well as a portion of their telephone and electric bills, from their gross income. Business-related expenses (e.g., postage, travel, and office supplies) may also be deducted, and work-related equipment (e.g., computer, fax machine) may be depreciated. (Because tax regulations governing self-employed persons are frequently revised, it's a good idea to check with an accountant or tax preparer before taking these deductions.)

The down side is that freelancers pay a high price for their freedom. They have no basic employee benefits: no sick days or paid vacations, no health insurance or workmen's compensation. They must provide for their own retirement. "I couldn't get sick, I couldn't go away," complained one former freelancer. "All I did was get fat, because I couldn't stay away from the refrigerator."

Freelancers also have to be able to tolerate a high degree of uncertainty. Publishing is a very volatile business; editors, divisions, and even houses come and go; every freelancer has had the experience of losing a client. "You have to be prepared to start over," says a textbook copyeditor, "and have the confidence to know that if you're good, you can always find work."

Freelancers suffer chronic anxiety on two counts: about having too much work, and about having too little. Editorial work is cyclical, driven by the two or three "lists" of new books a house publishes yearly. A freelance copyeditor may find herself working day and night for several weeks during a peak period. Then, abruptly, there are no more manuscripts until the next list and the next copyediting cycle comes around. Some freelancers grab all the work they can when it's available, then use the down time to accomplish other goals. Others diversify; when the copyediting cycle is over, they go on to proofreading or perhaps pick up an index or two. Still others beat the publishing blues by freelancing outside the book business. (See the section "Beyond Books" at the end of this chapter.)

"Where is my check?" Every freelancer has asked this anxious question. It's probably in the mail—or will be within four to six weeks. If the check doesn't arrive within a month after completing a job, the freelancer should call the publisher. Checks—and invoices—do get lost. For that reason (as well as for tax purposes), freelancers should keep careful financial records, including copies of every bill. Another occupational hazard of freelancing is feeling isolated. "You're cut off from your professional peers," one freelancer told us, "and if you live alone, from other people." One way to counter occasional loneliness is to reward yourself with dinner with a friend after a solid day's work. Another is to schedule breaks in the workday to run errands or take a stroll and so feel part of the human race. The telephone is the freelancers' lifeline, their personal and professional link to the outside world. And, if you're a freelancer who still doesn't have an answering machine, get one!

Many freelancers join organizations that allow them to network as well as to make social contacts. (Networking is important, since the recommendation of one respected freelancer is usually enough to get work for another.) Editorial Freelancers Association (71 West 23rd Street, Suite 1504, New York, NY 10010), which has more than a thousand members in the United States, publishes a bimonthly newsletter addressed specifically to freelancers' concerns and sponsors monthly programs, affinity groups, and workshops that treat every aspect of editorial freelancing. The Freelance Editorial Association (P.O. Box 835, Cambridge, MA 02238) publishes a quarterly newsletter and has established The Members' Network, a telephone service that puts members in touch with colleagues who can answer their questions. The Freelance Editors' Association of Canada (50 Devon Rd., Toronto, Ont., Canada M4E 2J7), headquartered in Toronto, has branches in Vancouver, Montreal, and Ottawa and also publishes a newsletter and sponsors courses and events for freelancers. (For more information on the courses offered by these organizations, see Chapter 8.)

Freelancers who live in the same area as the publishers they work for can also ease their sense of being cut off by developing personal relationships with their in-house contacts. Occasionally dropping off a job in person and saying hello to the managing editor also helps keep the freelancer's name in the forefront of that editor's mind, which is a plus when the next work cycle rolls around.

Getting Work

Breaking In

Publishing in general, and freelancing in particular, is a "who you know" business. Because of this, most freelancers believe that the best way to break in is to work for a while in-house. Working in-house gives the future freelancer experience—including feedback on his work from a senior staff member or copy chief—as well as the opportunity to develop professional contacts.

Once a freelancer has established himself as competent, reliable, and professional, a managing editor will often refer him to colleagues at other houses or other divisions within the same house. And if that editor changes jobs, she will usually continue to be a source of work. The freelancer will then have the option of working for both the original house and the one to which the editor has moved.

Is it possible to freelance without any prior in-house experience? The consensus of freelancers we interviewed is that it can be done, but it's much more difficult.

Begin, as usual, by doing your homework. There are excellent copyediting and proofreading guides on the market, including self-teaching manuals. In addition, many universities and professional organizations offer publishing-related courses (see Chapter 8). Taking such courses assures an aspiring freelancer of feedback on his work and also provides the opportunity for some preliminary networking.

Because proofreading is essentially a mechanical skill, it's probably the best place for a novice to start. All of us have done a little proofreading (Remember working for your high school newspaper? How about that letter you wrote yesterday, correcting your spelling before mailing it?). Many proofreaders graduate to copyediting by studying the copyedited manuscripts they've worked on. After they've picked up enough mistakes and omissions by the copyeditor, they gain the courage to ask their in-house contact for their first copyediting job. Others are very comfortable doing proofreading and continue to look for that work. Still others do both copyediting and proofreading, taking whatever is available.

How about indexing? Is it a tougher area to break into? Yes, but "once you're in, you're in," according to a veteran indexer. Because this isn't a field that appeals to everyone, good indexers are always in demand.

Like aspiring copyeditors and proofreaders, the aspiring indexer should begin by familiarizing herself with the discipline by reading up on the subject. She can also take an indexing course and, if possible, volunteer to do an index for a local association or organization. If the indexer lives in a university town, she might also offer to assist a professor in the preparation of an index for a scholarly book.

Before hiring an indexer, publishers usually require work

SUGGESTED FREELANCING SUPPLIES

1. The "basics": red pencils, flags, and erasers; reference sources (style manual, dictionary, etc.).
2. Telephone answering machine (with professional-sounding message); calculator (for figuring finances); typewriter or word processor for preparing style and query sheets and bills, and for retyping messy manuscript pages (see item 5).
3. Library card (either to a public or good private library).
4. Business cards and stationery.
5. (Optional) Computer and printer, if you can afford them*; a fax machine can also be useful.

*Since more and more editing work is being processed electronically, computers will eventually be a must for freelancers.

---

samples as well as two or three references. Once an indexer is known, word of mouth is usually enough to guarantee her as much work as she can handle.

The American Society of Indexers (P.O. Box 386, Port Aransas, TX 78373) publishes a bimonthly national newsletter, *Key Words*, and also provides its members with *The Indexer* (published twice a year), the British bible of indexing. The Society is *the* contact for indexers, keeping members up to date on indexing publications, computer software, and the doings of different chapters across the country.

Calling cold. So you've done your homework and now you're ready to look for work. But how do you get it if you have no contacts? You make the dreaded "cold" call.

Calling cold means telephoning a managing editor, copy chief, or production editor you don't know to ask for work. If this is too daunting, you may want to prepare the way by sending a query letter and resumé ahead of time. But the advantage of a preliminary call is that it can save you time and energy. If you find out right off that there's no work, you can move on to another possible source.

Before calling, you should do a little research to ascertain which houses you'd like to work for. *Literary Market Place* (*LMP*), which is available at most public libraries, lists publishers alphabetically and also groups them according to their type (trade or textbook, for instance) and their lists (nonfiction, children's books, etc.). *LMP*, an annual, often lists the names of managing editors and copy chiefs, but people move around so readily in publishing that the information is often out of date. This is another argument for calling before you write.

Book packagers—small, independent firms that handle almost every phase of book publishing—are also an excellent source of work for editorial freelancers. They rely heavily on freelance editors, copyeditors, and proofreaders, as well as writers, indexers, and photo researchers, in order to keep full-time staff to a minimum. Some, though not all, packagers are listed in *LMP*. The American Book Producers Association (ABPA) (160 Fifth Avenue, Suite 604, New York, NY 10010), the packagers' professional organization, will provide, on request, a list of its members and each packager's area of specialization (e.g., sports books, gardening books, and how-to's). Packagers range from the newly established "one-man band" to well-staffed outfits that have been around for years. If a packager isn't well known, it's wise for a freelancer to ask around to ascertain its reputation (read: solvency).

Even experienced freelancers have to make cold calls, usually when a work source suddenly dries up. If they have enough warning, many try to call while they're still busy— which means while they're still feeling positive rather than anxious. It's a trick beginners can learn from. How a freelancer handles herself over the phone is the first indication an editor has of her professionalism. Remember that sounding confident inspires confidence.

About resumés. The usual response to a cold call is "Send us your resumé." A resumé is a sales tool, so it's worth spending time to make it an effective one. If you're a beginner, you should stress any special expertise and any related experience. If you've freelanced before, your resumé should include a client list. A resumé should not list any or all jobs in chronological sequence, only those that are recent, and relevant to the work you're trying to get. Your educational history should be included, and if you have a degree in an area in which you'd like to work (e.g., a psychology B.A. and you want to edit books in the social sciences), you should mention this in your cover letter. Computer skills should be listed, along with the hardware and software you're familiar with. And be prepared to provide publishing references on request, if you have any.

For a beginner, an effective cover letter can help compensate for a lack of experience. So can demonstrated enthusiasm for and knowledge about the publisher to whom you are applying. Special interests may also give you a foot in the door. For example, a gourmet cook found a niche proofreading, then copyediting, cookbooks (he went on to write a cookbook of his own). In another instance, a recent graduate with a B.S. in physics used her degree to get work copyediting textbooks in the "hard" sciences (eventually she became an in-house editor).

A resumé and the accompanying letter should always be typed, not handwritten, and carefully checked for grammatical errors and typos. Both resumé and letter are samples of a freelancer's writing as well as her editing and proofreading skills. If the applicant fails this initial test, a managing editor won't bother giving her any other.

About two weeks after sending off a resumé, a freelancer should make a follow-up phone call. Hearing nothing back means nothing, either about you or your credentials. Managing editors are busy people—they depend on you to contact *them*. If you want your resumé to stay on top of the pile, you must keep reminding your in-house contacts that you are ready and willing to work.

Testing, one, two, three. Publishers often give out tests to prospective freelance copyeditors and proofreaders. The freelancer is allowed to take the test at home, and to use a style guide, a dictionary, and any other reference book he would use when working.

Be warned that no manuscript or page proof ever contains as many errors in style, grammar, and usage or typos as these tests. They are designed to drive freelancers crazy, and to make them worry afterward, "What did I miss?" The best way to proceed with such a test is slowly and thoroughly. Work through it once, then put it aside for a day, and approach it again with a fresh eye. Above all, follow directions carefully: If it's a proofreading test, don't copyedit it; if it's a copyediting test, don't rewrite it.

Some copyediting and proofreading guides offer sample tests, which can serve as a trial run and give you an idea of the kinds of problems you're likely to encounter. Sometimes publishers assign to prospective freelancers a project that also serves as a test; this is done more commonly for proofreading than for copyediting. Not only does this provide the potential employer a more accurate indication of an applicant's skills, it also allows the freelancer to be paid for the time and effort spent taking the test.

Exposing yourself.   Another way to reach potential clients is to advertise. Each of the freelance organizations described earlier in this chapter publishes a members' directory. Updated annually, the directories are offered not only to members but to anyone wishing to hire freelance editorial professionals. The Freelance Editorial Association *Yellow Pages* lists hundreds of freelancers from all over the United States. Both the Editorial Freelancers Association and The Freelance Editors' Association of Canada offer members a telephone service (called the Job Phone and Hotline, respectively). The services enable freelancers to match their skills against currently available jobs, posted by subscribing employers.

The trade magazine *Publishers Weekly* (249 West 17th Street, New York, NY 10010) has a "Resource Directory" that includes ads placed by editorial freelancers. (For current rates, contact *PW*'s advertising department.) The annual *Literary*

Market Place lists freelancers under "Editorial Services" without charge, as long as they can supply three publishing references to be included. Newcomers without experience might still find *LMP* useful since some of the editorial services listed farm out their overload work to other freelancers. A call to them might produce work.

Another relatively inexpensive way for freelancers to get their names out is to invest in business cards. The card should be simple and to the point, including the freelancer's name, address, and phone number, and her editorial specialty or specialties. Enterprising freelancers carry their cards even on social occasions. One rewrite specialist met a possible client at a dinner party and gave him her card. He called her for work the next day, "which he wouldn't have done if I hadn't had my cards—he was too tipsy to remember my name." The point is, you never know who you'll meet, and having a business card handy both facilitates networking and shows a freelancer's professionalism.

Fair pay and fair practice. Two useful publications address the questions of how much pay freelancers should expect for their services and what they should know about business dealings with clients.

Editorial Freelancers Association publishes a biannual *Rates Survey*, available to members, that offers a detailed business profile of EFA's members, including gross incomes of part-time and full-time freelancers; average length of time for payment; how often—and by how much—members raised rates. (In book publishing, freelance rates are generally set by the publisher, although there is often room to negotiate.) The survey provides an analysis of the payments members received for their services (categories include Publishers/Packagers; Corporate/Business; and Individual Clients; and skill areas range from Abstracting and Abridging to Copyediting and Writing).

The Freelance Editorial Association publishes a booklet entitled *Code of Fair Practice* that defines ethical standards and contract guidelines for editorial freelancers and clients.

The *Code* is a resource that helps freelancers negotiate agreements and promotes fair business practices. In addition, the Association's Fair Practice Committee helps members to resolve disputes with clients. Members can go to this committee for advice and advocacy if conflicts arise.

What Makes a Successful Freelancer?

As we've noted, some in-house experience is immensely helpful in launching a freelance career. Developing contacts is almost as important. And it goes without saying that, to be successful, freelancers must be competent in their area of expertise and capable of working under pressure.

The following qualities were also cited by freelancers as contributing to their success.

- You must be *disciplined*. One freelancer described discipline as "that sense of commitment that gets you to meet deadlines and do the best job you can."
- You must be *dependable*. Books are invariably produced on tight schedules with one stage following another, and editors prize freelancers who can be counted on to deliver their work on time and not jeopardize the schedule.
- You must be *secure*. Freelancers aren't praised for their work. Their reward is another assignment. As a freelancer, you have to be able to judge your own efforts—Have I done what was required to fulfill the assignment?—and be confident enough to call again to ask for another project.
- You must be *persistent*. Persistence is essential when a freelancer is initially trying to get work from a publisher. But even veterans check in frequently with their established contacts. A call from a freelancer letting a house know when she'll be free is always appreciated—and smart.
- You must be *assertive*. One of freelancers' biggest gripes is that publishers often don't give adequate—or accu-

---

SIX PRACTICAL POINTERS FOR FREELANCERS

1. Take care of your eyes and have them checked regularly.
2. Be sure to work in good light.
3. Be sure your work space is well ventilated.
4. Have a desk, or table, that affords enough space so you can spread out, and a comfortable chair that gives you good back support.
5. Take frequent breaks both to rest your eyes and to refresh your mind and body.
6. Know your own limits. Editorial freelancing requires intense concentration. Stop when you feel yours is falling off.

---

rate—instructions on a project. If halfway through a manuscript a "light edit" starts turning into rewriting, it's up to the freelancer to call and ask for clarification. "You're not only being professional, you're protecting yourself," a copyeditor advised. Her point was that a publisher may not want you to take the extra time—or their money—to do a "better" job.

- Finally, you must be *adaptable*. Freelancers have to be able to take in stride the ups and downs of publishing cycles—and of the publishing business itself. They must also be open to change and grasp opportunities to grow professionally. One such opportunity is to be found in the increasing computerization of publishing. Computer literacy is fast becoming a must for today's freelancers (see Chapter 7). One freelance copyeditor combined her editorial expertise and her computer skills and created her own national newsletter for copyeditors. An indexer who overcame her original computerphobia so that she could work in that field went on to establish a desktop publishing business of her own. The best advice we can offer freelancers is to think of yourselves as entrepreneurs who can adapt to changing circumstances and changing markets.

Beyond Books

Because our book is about book editing, our emphasis in this chapter has been on freelancing for book publishers. But magazines and newspapers also use editorial freelancers—in particular, copyeditors and proofreaders—as do many other businesses. Accounting firms, brokerage houses, law firms, and advertising agencies often farm out the editing of in-house organs (such as newsletters), annual reports, brochures, and articles (law and accounting firms in particular also use indexers). Pharmaceutical firms use proofreaders and copyeditors for many of their publications, including newsletters and press releases, as well as for preparing reports on drugs to be submitted for approval to the U.S. Food and Drug Administration. Medical ad agencies, which take on overload work for the pharmaceutical companies, need editors and writers to prepare written materials for conferences and to help turn presentations into papers, as well as to assist doctors in preparing articles for publication. Nonprofit organizations, government agencies, and educational institutions also hire freelancers to work on a variety of publications.

"Don't think books," advised an established freelancer who began her career as an assistant editor at an accounting firm. "Think the written word—think communication."

Corporations also tend to pay more than their publishing counterparts (see EFA *Rates Survey*). One area where this holds true is the field of medical editorial freelancing. A successful medical writer had this advice for freelancers interested in this potentially lucrative area: "First go to a medical library a day a week and read and read and read medical journals to develop an understanding of the terminology and methodology, and to find out whether you want to do such dry work. Then try to get in-house experience with a medical publisher, which is easier than starting with a pharmaceutical company or medical ad agency."

Working for medical publishers will give you a foundation for freelancing for the pharmaceutical companies and

ad agencies, and—especially if you move up to be a writer—
that's where the better money is.

Of course, freelancers work for love as well as money.
Although trade book publishers are notorious for paying
among the lowest rates, many freelancers find that working on fiction and nonfiction has its own rewards. It's really
a question of finding what suits you—and what you're
suited to. For instance, a freelance trade book copyeditor
who loves writing for its own sake might find medical editing too narrow and predictable. But according to one medical copyeditor, knowing what to expect was precisely what
she liked about her work. "The problem with trade books,"
she complained, "is that every one's different."

As any freelancer will tell you, being out there on your own
isn't always easy. In editorial freelancing, perhaps even more
than in any other profession, it's important to do what you
like and to like what you do.

Chapter 7

Electronic Editing Today and Tomorrow

by Linda Joan Brittain

Ever since the advent of computer technology, there has been talk about how it will revolutionize the publishing industry, simplifying both the editing and production of books—and perhaps even eliminating books as we know them altogether. Books are still very much with us, although, as we shall see in the last section of this chapter, the manner and medium in which they are produced and distributed are already undergoing massive change. Computers, with their enormous capacity to store, retrieve, manipulate, reproduce, and transmit information, have already had an enormous impact on publishing. Most notably their use has allowed publishers to keep more of the typesetting function in-house, in some cases bypassing the typesetter completely and taking the author's keystrokes—or those of an in-house word processing operator—all the way to film or camera-ready copy to be used by the printer.

When typesetters are eliminated, the production process is known as desktop publishing. For newspapers, desktop publishing is a natural and is now the norm; newspapers are produced more quickly and efficiently than before because everyone involved in the process, from reporters to designers to editors, is hooked into the same computerized

Linda Joan Brittain, who has a Ph.D. in social psychology, is an assistant director and computer consultant at Health & Hospitals Corporation in New York City. She previously worked in publishing, both in editorial and as permissions director at Farrar, Straus & Giroux.

Irene Gunther contributed to the research and writing of this chapter.

system, and copy is transmitted back and forth electronically without ever appearing on paper until the newspaper is printed. Books are, however, a different matter. Each is a separate entity, with its own set of editorial and production problems; each comes from a different source (which could be the author's computer, word processor, typewriter, or even pen). The current consensus in publishing seems to be that production decisions still have to be made on a case-by-case basis.

In this chapter we will focus on the computer's use—and its potential—in relation to two main categories of editors: acquiring editors, who can now take advantage of computerized databases[1] to research or evaluate book ideas, and editors (line editors and copyeditors) who work directly on authors' manuscripts. We will also touch upon the future of electronic publishing and its impact on the editing process.

The Computer in the Editing Process

How do editors use computers today? How has new technology changed their jobs?

It is the rare publishing house that hasn't yet provided its editorial staff some access to personal computers (PCs), even if they have to share the equipment. Many editors use a personal computer and word processing software much as they once used a typewriter: to produce letters, memos, reports, perhaps make notes on current and future projects, and so on. Others, such as managing editors and production editors, use scheduling software to monitor book production schedules, and still others take advantage of spreadsheet programs to calculate costs and profit margins.

In addition, catalog and jacket copy, form letters (including rejection letters to authors), permission requests, and many other items are computer generated. Forms and docu-

---

[1] The word "database" refers to any collection of information that is stored electronically.

ments are standardized and stored in a computer, making revisions easier, which translates into savings of time and money for the publisher.

More directly related to the editing process is the use of a computer database. A database is an electronic information storage system that allows material to be organized in different ways for different purposes. It is of particular value for large projects that contain vast amounts of data, such as encyclopedias and dictionaries, and those that are regularly updated and revised, such as almanacs and various kinds of catalogs. One simple function a computer could perform with a database would be to find and list in alphabetical order all of the contributors to an encyclopedia yearbook; from a dictionary database the computer could pull out and print all entries relating to a particular subject—for example, political parties or musical instruments—so that they could be edited as a group; or the computer could search a database for all cross-references so that the format of each one could be changed with a few keystrokes, using a global command. Revising products such as general encyclopedias, in which the basic format and a large percentage of the text usually remain unchanged from one edition to the next, is also made easier by the use of a database.

The use of computer technology has lagged in one area of publishing: To date, it has not had a major impact on the time it takes to turn an author's manuscript into a bound book—still, on average, nine months to a year. This is not, however, the fault of computers; the technology is available to cut down production time drastically (some books on hot topics, or that are otherwise time sensitive, *are* being produced in as little as four to five weeks). But in most cases, the backing and forthing of the editing process, the interrelationships among design, editing, and production departments, the role of the author, and the sheer mass of detail involved in producing a book all contribute to making the process a slow one.

Editing on Screen

As anyone who has used a word processor knows, editing on a computer screen has certain advantages over editing on paper. Line editors and copyeditors can add, delete, change, or rearrange text with a few simple keystrokes; problems with hard-to-read or messy handwriting or with lack of space to insert new copy are eliminated. If the editor decides that a set of items needs to be alphabetized or that a list should be sorted according to different criteria, the computer can do it in seconds.

When a change must be made throughout a manuscript—for instance, if a place name has been spelled incorrectly or inconsistently, or British spellings of certain words have to be changed to American spellings—a global search will pick up every instance so that the editor can make the changes or else instruct the computer to make them automatically. Indeed, whenever the editor's task is a relatively tedious, mechanical one that applies to all or a substantial part of the manuscript, the computer will always perform it more accurately than a human being, no matter how experienced, because its attention doesn't wander.

The spellchecking function built into most word processing software can also be useful, as long as the editor remembers that these programs pick up only misspelled words. A correctly spelled word that is the *wrong* word—for example, "capital" when "capitol" was intended, or "souse" instead of "spouse"—will not be identified.

Grammar-checking software programs such as Grammatik, Editor, and PowerEdit can help editors and proofreaders find lapses in usage, grammar, and punctuation and ease the burden of checking for opening and closing quotation marks, parentheses, brackets, and braces. But each of the grammar checkers currently on the market has its own quirky limitations. For instance, the period in "Mr." may be mistaken for a sentence-ending period and result in a frustrating query from the computer. A more general drawback to the current generation of grammar checkers is that they are programmed to impose one of a variety of writing styles (business, technical, general correspondence) on the text being checked, and the style may not be appropriate to the work at hand. At this point, we can recommend the use of grammar checkers only to catch mechanical errors.

The Electronic Manuscript

So, how commonly do editors edit manuscripts on a computer? It's a hard question to answer; it varies from publisher to publisher, from book to book. In the case of publications such as reference works, where a considerable proportion of the writing is done in-house, a lot of editing (as well as writing) will occur at the computer. But for most other books, there are problems arising from the mechanics of editing that have not yet been satisfactorily resolved by available computer hardware and software.

Many authors now create their work on computers, and some submit their completed manuscripts to publishers on disks. Theoretically, the manuscript could be transferred to an in-house computer (or even transmitted electronically from the author's computer to that of the publisher using an online electronic mail [E-mail] service), then edited, designed, proofread, corrected, and sent to the typesetter—or directly to the printer—without ever appearing on paper. This would result in savings for the publisher of both time and money. In practice, however, limitations cut into these potential economies.

For starters, the publisher will want the author to prepare the manuscript in a particular way. Some publishers will request that all text, including headings, footnotes, and bibliographies, be double-spaced and free of any special typesetting codes (e.g., codes indicating that text should be indented, centered, italicized, boldfaced, or printed in a specific typeface or font size). Other publishers will provide authors with instructions detailing the kinds of codes they should use, in effect asking the author to do part of the typesetter's job. One such set of instructions is contained in the *Chicago Guide to Preparing Electronic Manuscripts.*[2] But following such precise instructions often presupposes a degree of computer sophistication—and of attention to detail—that authors may not have (or wish to have).

For example, few authors are equipped to format satisfactorily such manuscript elements as lists, graphs, and tables, or numerous footnotes. College textbook publishers, therefore, generally find it more cost-efficient to send a complex or highly technical manuscript that requires heavy coding directly to the typesetter in hard-copy form rather than to submit an author-prepared disk. Many typesetters have special software to facilitate the handling of such elements as chemical formulas or mathematical equations.

If, as often happens, the author submits an electronic manuscript with codes that are incompatible with those used by the publisher, an in-house staffer will have to "uncode" and reformat it. When the manuscript is predominantly straight text—a novel, for instance—reformatting is a simple and relatively inexpensive matter. In the case of a complex book, though, the costs could be high enough to outweigh the potential savings of working in the electronic medium.

One solution to the babel would be for all publishers and typesetters to adopt a single standard for coding electronic manuscripts for the printer. Such a standard, called Standard Generalized Markup Language (SGML), has been developed and is used by many academic journals and scientific publications. But since many publishers have already developed and are satisfied with their own electronic manuscript coding systems, the industrywide adoption of SGML may take a long time.

Another potential barrier to electronic editing is the lack of compatibility between the operating system the author uses and the one used by his or her publisher. As anyone who has worked on a personal computer knows, there are

[2] *Chicago Guide to Preparing Electronic Manuscripts.* Chicago: University of Chicago Press, 1987.

several kinds of personal computers on the market, which run on different operating systems. The two best-known types of PCs are the IBM and IBM-compatibles and the Macintosh series. The IBMs and compatibles commonly use some version of PC-DOS (Personal Computer–Disk Operating System—MS-DOS is the most prevalent), while the Macintoshes utilize an operating system with two components called System and Finder (or MultiFinder).

For a long time, documents and files created on one type of operating system could not be easily transferred to and manipulated in the other. Recent developments in software and hardware, however, have made it possible to switch relatively seamlessly from one operating system to the other and to work in whichever environment is best suited to the tasks to be performed. (Most people find the PC-DOS system easier to use for word processing functions such as writing and editing but consider the Mac more efficient for graphics-related functions such as design and artwork.)

Incompatibility between software programs may also add to costs. If the author's word processing software is different from the publisher's, the disk will have to be converted so that it can be worked on in-house. This is less of a problem than it used to be: Subprograms that convert files from one commonly used word processing software system to another have been developed and are now a basic feature of most word processing packages.

As yet unresolved—and more crucial—is the question of how to review editing that has been done on screen. As a manuscript passes through the various stages of editing—from line editor to copyeditor, to author, typesetter, and proofreader, and back to editor and author for final checking—it is close to impossible, with standard word processing programs, to see whose hand has made what changes, and at what stage.

There are already some partial solutions, and others are on the horizon. For example, some software allows the user to split the screen and compare two versions of a document side by side. Some word processing packages have a red-lining or highlighting function that can be used to make notes, suggest corrections, ask questions, and so on. While highlighted sections cannot be printed, they can be read by another editor on screen, and also by the author if he or she has compatible software.

Beyond that, only a few software programs exist that are geared specifically to editing and that enable editors to make changes that stand out from the original text. A recent entry into this market is called PenEdit (from Advanced Pen Technologies). The flat-screen monitor weighs about five pounds and is the size of a notebook. The editor writes directly on the screen using a special magnetic pen, and her corrections and annotations appear in a scriptlike font that resembles handwriting, so that the author or another editor can see what has been done. PenEdit also allows editors to do many things they do with regular word processing software, such as inserting or moving copy or making global changes. The snag is the high price (about $6,500 for the software and hardware together), which will likely prompt most editing departments to stick with their colored pencils and paper, or the awkwardness of existing word processing software, at least for now. But new devices will no doubt be developed and prices will drop, making electronic editing more feasible and economical in the near future.

According to Richard Snyder, formerly chairman of Simon & Schuster, although most author submissions are still on paper, "As society changes, authors will demand that they give us the book electronically and won't submit to publishers who can't use those capabilities."[3]

It should be noted, however, that even with new editing software, many editors will be loath to relinquish entirely their longtime relationship with the printed page. They feel the need to look at words on paper, they say, to leaf through an article or chapter after they've finished editing it. This allows them to check the flow of language and sequence of

---

[3] "The Wiring of Simon & Schuster," *Publishers Weekly*, June 1, 1992, p. 34.

ideas, as well as to find errors they might have overlooked on the computer screen.

The Computer as Research Tool

Many people may still think the primary purpose of computers, especially large ones, is to serve as giant calculators that can do complex mathematics extremely quickly, and indeed that's how many scientists use them. However, computers of any size also excel at storing information for later retrieval and at comparing items of data, then copying and rearranging them in a different order. Thus, one task for which computers are ideally suited is to sort through enormous amounts of data to find a common thread.

Editors can capitalize on this storing, searching, and sorting capacity in a variety of ways. As we have discussed elsewhere (see Chapter 4), the editor's memory is a vital asset. A good memory enables acquiring editors to remember what they've seen and heard, to keep up with current events and trends in publishing, and to keep track of new ideas and novel approaches. But since no editor can retain everything he or she sees or learns, storing some of it in a computer can be a valuable supplement to memory.

Using Library Databases

Organizing her thoughts about a possible book, whether it is her own idea or one submitted by a prospective author, is only the first step for the acquiring editor. To decide whether the project is worth pursuing, she must do more research.

She may need, for example, to ascertain how much information is readily available on the topic and how current it is; she will want to look at similar books already published and project the size of the market for the one she has in mind. The local library is the obvious place to begin her search.

Because standardized codes (alphabets and numbers) were first developed to record and preserve data, such as the number of jars of grain harvested during the previous year, the amount of information that has been gathered and stored in one form or another is too vast to comprehend. Much of this knowledge is contained in some standard form—books, periodicals, newsletters, pamphlets—and is preserved in libraries. Sometimes, to save space, particularly in the case of bulky newspapers and periodicals, libraries have transferred the information onto microfilm. These days, however, more and more data are being stored electronically on computer disks, the most economical form of storage in terms of space. This is particularly true since the advent of CD-ROM technology.

CD-ROM stands for Compact Disk–Read Only Memory, the last part of which means that the data on such a disk can be accessed and retrieved by the user but cannot be changed or edited in any way. The storage capacity of a CD-ROM is tremendous; besides digitized visual and aural materials, a single disk can store approximately 250,000 to 300,000 pages of text. One CD-ROM (which is the same size as an audio CD) can, for example, store the printed information from an entire encyclopedia, or the complete works of Shakespeare, or the multivolume *Oxford English Dictionary*.

When the acquiring editor steps into the research department of any major public library, she will probably find, in addition to its book-filled shelves, rows and rows of computers, some with printers attached. Some of these computers contain a computerized version of the library's card catalogs. The editor could, for example, ask the computer to sort through a library's holdings to find every book or article published in English in the past twenty years dealing with energy-efficient alternatives for home heating that can be installed by the do-it-yourself homeowner. This would help the editor determine the potential market for a new book on this subject.

She might begin her research by going to a database called *Books in Print Plus*, in which all currently available books are listed by author, subject, and title. Typing in a few words to delineate the topic and letting the computer search for relevant titles is much quicker than leafing through the printed version of this material—and the information is likely to be more up to date. And, rather than sitting and taking notes with pencil and pad, she can get a printed copy of the titles of interest to her and then move on to the next step.

To look for articles on her subject, she may go next to the electronic version of *Readers' Guide to Periodical Literature*. She may also search the *Biography Index*, which contains citations to biographical material drawn from almost three thousand periodicals, or the *Art Index*, which cites articles covering important developments in art, architecture, graphic design, and so on. She can access articles from the *New York Times* database, which contains the full text of that newspaper for the preceding two years, and is updated monthly. Or she may go to the *British Newspaper Index on CD-ROM*, which indexes major British newspapers. Other available databases include a poetry index, a social sciences index, and various religion indexes; and there are many more.

Note that editors who have modems can in some cases tap into many databases without having to go to the library. This is especially true of academic writers with access to university libraries.

CD-ROM Goes to the Office

As more and more basic reference materials have become available in CD-ROM format, editorial departments have begun to install these disks on their own personal computers, or computer networks, so that some editors can now do at least part of their research without leaving their desks. They can check, say, the accuracy of a title in *Books in Print*, the name of an agent or publisher in *Literary Market Place*, or biographical data on a well-known scientist in Marquis's

Who's Who right at their computers. Reference works such as dictionaries, encyclopedias, and atlases may also be on the network. Having ready access to this kind of information can be a timesaver not just for acquiring editors but also for copyeditors, researchers, and proofreaders—anyone who needs to check a fact.

Information Retrieval Services

If the local library's offerings are too limited in scope, the search for information could be expanded to encompass information retrieval services. Such services operate very large computers to store tremendous amounts of data on subjects ranging from the everyday to the arcane. The largest of them provide access to hundreds of different databases.

Some editorial departments, particularly those of reference book publishers, which need more specialized data than current CD-ROM databases can provide, subscribe to one or another of these services. An encyclopedia publisher, for example, may subscribe to Nexis/Lexis, an online service whose database includes hundreds of newspapers and periodicals, both in the United States and overseas, many of which are updated daily. Editors or fact checkers can use this electronic library to get ideas for articles, to fill in missing information, or to do last-minute updates on, for example, a pending criminal case, a political crisis in the making, or the latest sports results.

Conducting an online database search has several advantages over doing a search at the local library. With the possible exception of the Library of Congress, the scope of major online databases is larger than any library's, and the data are updated more often. Moreover, data are available (through a personal computer, modem, and telephone line linkup) twenty-four hours a day, every day; no library can match those hours. And an electronic search with a powerful host computer can be done more quickly than with a smaller computer (and is obviously much faster than a manual search of card files). On the other hand, online databases can be costly—users generally pay a subscription fee and are also charged for the time they are connected to the host computer. As a result, editors generally employ these databases sparingly, and only after in-house sources of information have been exhausted or when a deadline demands a quick answer.

Dialog Information Services, Inc., a subsidiary of Lockheed, is the world's leading information retrieval service, with more than 300 databases. The information in these databases is provided by well-known corporations, associations, publishers, and government agencies. Knowledge-Index consists of a subset of about 50 of the Dialog databases and costs substantially less to access during evening and weekend hours. Both services have available a number of standard references, including *Grolier's Academic American Encyclopedia*, *Books in Print*, and Marquis's *Who's Who*.

The Dow Jones News/Retrieval Service consists mostly of business publications like *The Wall Street Journal*, so it is primarily for business users. However, it is an excellent source of information on current events and recent history, and it offers reviews of current books and movies.

Newsnet is also a business-oriented service. Editors might find its coverage of publishing and broadcasting newsletters of greatest interest.

Another electronic library, called World Wide Web, is an international collection of databases accessible through Internet, a global system of computer networks. At one time the Web was almost solely the province of research scientists, and Internet users consisted of several thousand computer scientists, engineers, and programmers who freely shared online material with one another. Once information retrieval programs like Gopher and Mosaic were introduced, however, several million PC users rushed to explore the Internet and the databases available through it. If their place of business or university wasn't connected directly to the Internet, they dialed up via a commercial online information service to pursue data that are mostly free. Data range from items in the catalogs of the Library of Congress and many American and foreign university libraries, in federal government archives, museums, and NASA computers (e.g., satellite photos), to juicy bits in the latest, hottest online scandal sheets.

For other database directories, contact either the Information Industry Association at (202) 639–8260 or Knowledge Industry Publications, Inc., at (914) 328–9157.

Finally, we need to mention that, rather than conduct database searches themselves, editors may choose to hire a freelancer called an information broker to do this work for them. The information broker is already familiar with various locally available and special online databases and has the expertise required to track down information as quickly as possible. Such brokers are listed in telephone company Yellow Pages and in the directory *Information Industry Market Place* (Bowker).

Bulletin Board Services (BBS)

Networking is an important part of the acquiring editor's job, whether with agents, colleagues, authors, or others in the publishing field. Most of the time networking involves face-to-face or telephone contact, but it can also be done electronically, through a bulletin board service, or BBS.

A BBS is the electronic equivalent of the kind of bulletin board that can be found in community centers, supermarkets, or local stores. It serves as a repository for the most current information on topics that may be of interest to its regular users.

Let's suppose an editor is intrigued by a proposal but doesn't know enough about the subject matter to evaluate its potential for a book. He may ask reviewers to read the proposal and give him an opinion as to its worth. But what if he doesn't know any readers informed enough about the topic to render a judgment?

If he's a computer buff, he may decide to tap into a local or national electronic bulletin board service, which he can access any time through his PC, modem, and phone line. Typically, local electronic bulletin board services are established and operated by computer enthusiasts looking to connect with other PC users who have similar interests—in computing, politics, the sciences, the arts, travel, lifestyles, or any topic imaginable. The operator of a BBS, who is known as a "sysop" (system operator), may set up special interest groups (SIGs) to make it easier for regular callers to communicate with those who share similar interests.

Members of a SIG can use their PC keyboard to type messages, which are transmitted over the phone line to the BBS's host computer. The host computer then acts as a kind of centralized switchboard, relaying those messages to the appropriate parties. Messages can also be posted in the general bulletin board area of a BBS to be read by any other caller.

Thus, our acquiring editor with a specific book subject in mind could post a message requesting callers to respond if they are interested in writing such a book or in acting as a consultant or reviewer, or if they can recommend someone with the necessary expertise. Obviously, as with contacts made through nonelectronic means, the editor will have to check respondents' credentials to see if they are suitable for the assignment.

An Electronic Notebook

As we mentioned earlier, many editors may use a personal computer as a glorified notebook in which they jot down ideas and impressions, comments overheard during lunch or on the street, an individual's name and area of expertise, and anything else that might one day result in a salable product.

When she is out of the office and on the run, the editor may find it both helpful and time saving to enter her notes into one of the simplest kinds of computers. Known as a personal scheduler/organizer, this electronic gadget is relatively inexpensive and slim enough and light enough to fit into a shirt pocket or a small purse. The more sophisticated organizers feature a decent-sized database in which to enter a daily schedule, a personal phone directory, and any notes. When shopping around for this type of device, the editor should look for one that, with the appropriate connectors, makes it possible to transfer data from the organizer to a desktop computer. This will allow her, at a later time, to work with her notes in comfort on a full-sized keyboard rather than on the organizer's more cramped one.

A Look Ahead

The Move to Multimedia

As we try to visualize the state of book publishing in the twenty-first century, we anticipate that, in addition to changes in the production process, the distinctions between different types of publishing media—books, videotapes, CD-ROMs, and so on—will blur, and multimedia packages will become commonplace. The medium will be the CD-ROM, on which written text may be combined with pictures—stills, animations, or video graphics—and sounds, including music and speech. At present, CD-ROMs come in three varieties: Some contain only text, some are multimedia, and others are interactive.

Software stores already have shelves and shelves of CD-ROMs, the extent of which goes far beyond the reference books to which we've referred so far. In fact, the range of subjects is enormous.

Do you want to learn a foreign language? How to play a musical instrument? Would you like to view artistic masterpieces, visit a national park, play an interactive video game? It's all there for you. At present, most CD-ROM packages are put together by software companies, but publishers are now beginning to enter the field.

Interactive CD-ROMs. An interesting aspect of multimedia publications is a technique called *hypertext*, which invisibly links key words to other words and information in a way similar to how people think—by association. When the reader selects one of the key words, he or she activates the hypertext linkages so as to reveal any associated information (e.g., pictures, sounds, or other text). Thus, hypertext allows the user to interact with the reading material and so access information on related topics—a feature that is especially useful for someone conducting research. Hypertext is also used in interactive video games; your choice of move dictates what happens next in the game you're playing with the computer.

The major hindrance at the moment to the full development of interactive multimedia publishing is that there are several kinds of CD-ROM players, or systems, on the market, which use different—and incompatible—technologies. Unsure which hardware format will become the standard, consumers are still somewhat reluctant to invest in a CD-ROM player. (This is reminiscent of what happened with the early videocassette players, when VHS was competing with Betamax.) However, this situation should resolve itself before too long when one format or another manages to gain favor with a majority of software developers.

The Computer in the Classroom

Many college students now have their own personal computers, and, for those who don't, computers are readily available on most campuses. These are beginning to be used for purposes other than writing term papers; for example, some professors use them in interactive language or science courses.

Another recent development—which may make the traditional college textbook old hat—is the arrival of "books on demand." Pioneering this concept is McGraw-Hill, Inc., which in 1990 introduced a system called Primis (for Prime Information System). Primis is an electronic database containing college textbook material that allows professors to customize the books they use. They can pick and choose from a variety of (overwhelmingly McGraw-Hill) texts and supplementary materials such as tests and study guides to suit the needs of each class and even of individual students. Besides textbooks, Primis also offers some fiction and non-fiction works. A teacher of comparative literature could, for example, request a package to illuminate the exposition of the concepts of good and evil that would include a Plato dialog, one act of *Hamlet*, and a chapter from a Dostoevsky novel. Such a package would save students the expense of buying three separate books for a course. Sales representatives work with professors and help them assemble the material they want, and the individualized orders then go to a printer. It is anticipated that in time high-tech, high-speed printing software systems (now very expensive, but expected to come down in price) will allow colleges and universities to print these tailor-made books right on campus, possibly within hours.

Ziff-Davis, which, like McGraw-Hill, publishes computer magazines and provides online information services accessible by modem to PC users, is also exploring the world of multimedia publishing, as is the publishing giant Simon & Schuster.

The Way We'll Communicate?

In the near future, the computer may well become a regular household item, as common perhaps as telephones, radios, TVs, and VCRs. Through a PC and its accoutrements, we will be able to read text, view pictures, and communicate with others on a myriad of subjects with a few keystrokes, a few clicks of a mouse button, or a few taps of a stylus. We will also be able to share the information we produce almost instantaneously, not just by talking about it but by sending and receiving text and graphic files through electronic linkages.

You, the reader, probably will not be taking a palmtop computer to the beach tomorrow to read the latest summer sizzler. But, the day may come when, instead of buying books or subscribing to magazines and newspapers, you'll be able—for a fee—to read or view any material of special interest to you by turning on a computer and dialing a phone number. Your printer, of course, will be available to make a hard copy of any item you wish to refer to regularly.

The Editor of Tomorrow

Where do all these trends leave the editor? Will he or she play a smaller role in book publishing?

We don't think so. As writers find that they can publish and distribute their own work themselves using their computers, desktop publishing software, and telecomputing (e.g., BBSs), more of them may choose this option, especially if they are writing for a small, specialized audience. But regardless of the medium, electronic or print, the great majority of books will still need editors to ensure that a certain level of quality in the writing and a consistent style are maintained.

We expect that editors will do more of their work on computers as better text-editing software is developed and there is greater compatibility between systems. (Paradoxically, as stylus technology is perfected, book editors may also find themselves making changes the "old-fashioned" way—not by applying pen to paper, though, but by using a stylus, or electronic pen, on the surface of a computer screen or pad.)

Computers have already blurred the lines between the functions of editors, typesetters, production personnel, and even authors. This blurring is likely to continue. Typesetting functions, as noted earlier, are increasingly being performed inside the publishing house. Meanwhile, desktop publishing software packages and standardized book designs are turning production and editing personnel into designers, thus diminishing the need for in-house design staff and even for freelance designers.

Editors, in particular, are already learning new skills as they work on computer screens. Besides correcting grammar, style, and usage, they may sometimes find themselves inserting codes and laying out pages, including making decisions about the placement of illustrations. Freelance editors, too, will have to be computer literate, able to edit on their own PCs and return their work to the publisher either on disk or via electronic mail.

Working with electronic books will change the editor's job in more fundamental ways, according to Robert Lynch, the director of Primis. Lynch believes that editors will be more, not less, important, in the future—and that they will have to rethink the way books are put together.

The fact that electronically created textbooks and similar materials can be updated and revised almost instantly to keep up with the latest developments means that editors working in this medium will also have to keep up to date in their field. They will also have to become familiar with the potential of computer technology and help their authors understand it better. Even if they are involved only with the text portion of a multimedia product, editors must be aware of how text interrelates with other elements and find innovative ways to present information.

In conclusion, it seems clear that computers will profoundly alter the way books are published. New technological advancements and new applications for book production will surely continue to be developed at a rapid rate, with today's ooh-aah technology dating quickly, and editors will need to keep abreast.

Indeed, the time may come when computers will not only help in the editing and production of books—they may also write books themselves. A 1993 story in the *New York Times*[4] described how, over a period of ten years, Scott French programmed a computer, using an artificial intelligence soft-

[4]Steve Lohr, "Potboiler Springs from Computer's Loins," *New York Times*, July 3, 1993, p. A1.

ware program, to write a Jacqueline Susann–style romance novel called *Just This Once*. French admits that both he and the computer each wrote only about one-quarter of the book, collaborating on the rest in a back-and-forth exchange that took much longer than had French written the book alone. Still, this incident just may be a sign of things to come.

Annotated Bibliography

Books and Articles

Banks, Michael A. *The Modem Reference*. New York: Brady (Simon & Schuster), 1988. A solid text on telecomputing that provides detailed explanations and descriptions of modems, communication software packages, bulletin board services and special interest groups, information retrieval services and research databases, electronic mail, and commercial online services such as Prodigy and CompuServe.

Eglowstein, Howard. "Applying the power of the pen." *BYTE*, vol. 18, no. 8, July 1993, pp. 132–40. Discusses several basic word processing, spreadsheet, and scheduler software packages for pen computing—in which the user applies a stylus to a screen to give computer commands and to enter information.

Hedtke, John V. *Using Computer Bulletin Boards*, 2nd ed. New York: MIS: Press (a subsidiary of Henry Holt), 1992. An easy-to-read, thorough introduction to BBSs and how to access them.

Kimble, Jim. *How to Get Started with Modems*. San Diego, Calif.: Computer Publishing Enterprises, 1989. An elementary guide to modems, electronic bulletin boards, and online services.

Walter, Russ. *The Secret Guide to Computers*, 17th ed. Somerville, Mass.: Russ Walter, 1993. A self-publication that is updated every year, this is an informative and humorous basic guide to everything you ever wanted to know about computers and includes the author's phone number to get additional information and advice about buying hardware and software. Toward this end, you might also wish to consult recent lab report articles in computer magazines such as *BYTE*, *MacUser*, *PC/Computing*, *PC World*, and *MacWEEK*.

Database Searches and Electronic Networking

To find the bulletin board services that are operating in your area, look at the comprehensive nationwide listing that is published every other month (beginning in January) in *Computer Shopper* magazine.

Examples of commercial online services are: CompuServe (owned by H&R Block), MCI Mail (for electronic mail), Dialog (for research), Nexis (for news), Lexis (for legal information), GEnie, Delphi, Prodigy (owned by Sears), and America Online.

Chapter 8

Tools of the Trade
and How to Use Them

At the Editor's Elbow

If you're a beginning editor, in particular a freelancer with limited resources, chances are you'll have on your desk only the basic editing tools—a couple of lined pads, a few well-sharpened colored pencils with erasers, removable self-stick notes or other flags in different sizes. And, of course, a dictionary and a style manual.

As an in-house staff editor you may also have access to an in-house library with a good selection of reference books; as a freelancer, you'll find a valuable resource in your local public library. But before taking a step away from your desk, know your dictionary and style manual and familiarize yourself with their contents. You'll probably be surprised to find out how much information you have right at your fingertips—and how much time you can save by being aware of it.

You will, of course, use your dictionary to check the meanings of words, their spellings and correct division into syllables, and sometimes to look for synonyms. But you should also be aware of the considerable reference information most college dictionaries now contain. For example, brief biographies of famous people past and present can often supply basic information such as a birth date, saving the step of going to a biographical or historical dictionary; geographical entries allow you to locate places and check their spellings without turning to an atlas; lists of signs and symbols provide a quick check if you are working on technical material; tables of weights and measures, metric conversion tables, lists of common abbreviations or of foreign words and phrases also come in handy.

Similarly, your style manual, beyond answering basic questions such as, "Do I italicize the name of a TV show or put it in quotation marks?" or "How many ellipsis points do I use at the end of a sentence?," may provide an overview of the publishing industry, a section on typography, general information on grammar and usage, or a list of some foreign alphabets.

Finally, in a world in which maps are being constantly redrawn as countries come apart and new ones are formed, an up-to-date atlas is a useful thing to have on one's desk, in addition to a dictionary and style manual.

The annotated bibliography that follows is divided into subject areas such as "Book Editing," "Style Manuals," "Dictionaries," and "Books on Writing."

Annotated Bibliography

Book Publishing

GENERAL

Books in Print. New Providence, N.J.: R. R. Bowker. Published annually. An editorial office must, which lists all books currently in print; organized by author, title, and subject. Used by editors (and authors) to check what's in print on any subject, and who wrote it; available to consult in many bookstores.

British Books in Print: The Reference Catalogue of Current Literature. London and New York: J. Whitaker & Sons and R. R. Bowker. Published annually. British version of *Books in Print*.

The Bowker Annual of Library and Book Trade Information. New Providence, N.J.: R. R. Bowker. Published annually. An almanac that surveys the book industry.

Dessauer, John P. *Book Publishing: A Basic Introduction*. New, expanded ed. New York: Continuum, 1989. A solid and useful overview of the publishing industry and how it works. Excellent introduction for students.

Geiser, Elizabeth A., and Arnold Dolin, with Gladys S. Topkis. *The Business of Book Publishing*. Boulder, Colo.: Westview Press, 1986. A comprehensive book about all areas of book publishing. Particularly useful to those contemplating a career in the field.

Landau, Sidney I. *Dictionaries: The Art and Craft of Lexicography*. New York: Cambridge University Press, 1989. All you need to know about dictionaries and dictionary making; authoritative, comprehensive, lucid, and often witty.

Literary Market Place (LMP). New Providence, N.J.: R. R. Bowker. Published annually. Directory of the book business, listing publishers and editors, literary agents, editorial services, etc.

Potter, Clarkson N. *Who Does What and Why in Book Publishing: Writers, Editors, and Money Men*. New York: Carol Publishing, 1990. A look at book publishing from three different standpoints. A very readable, occasionally opinionated, inside-industry look.

Tebbel, John. *Between Covers: The Rise & Transformation of Book Publishing in America*. New York: Oxford University Press, 1987. A one-volume version of Tebbel's monumental four-volume work.

———. *A History of Book Publishing in the United States*. Vol. 4. *The Great Change, 1940–1980*. New York: R. R. Bowker, 1981. A useful, straightforward chronicle of changes in the publishing industry.

BOOK PRODUCTION

Lee, Marshall. *Bookmaking: The Illustrated Guide to Design, Production, Editing*. 2nd ed. New York: R. R. Bowker, 1980. The classic in the field; in-depth discussions of design, production, and editing, and the way they interface.

Pocket Pal: A Graphic Arts Production Handbook. 13th ed. New York: International Paper Co., 1983. A compact, inexpensive guide to every aspect of production. A longtime favorite.

BOOK EDITING

Boston, Bruce O., ed. *STET! Tricks of the Trade for Writers and Editors*. Arlington, Va.: Editorial Experts, 1986. A collection of articles from *The Editorial Eye*, Editorial Experts' newsletter. Subjects range from "Commandments for Copyeditors" to "Tips on Proposal Writing" to "How to Hire a Proofreader" and "How to Recognize a Good Index."

Butcher, Judith M. *Copy-editing: The Cambridge Handbook Desk Edition.* 3rd ed. Cambridge, England: Cambridge University Press, 1991. A classic British guide, useful on this side of the Atlantic as well. Covers all aspects of the editorial processes involved in converting text or disk to printed page; with a wealth of clear examples, checklists.

Gross, Gerald. *Editors on Editing.* 3rd ed. New York: Grove Press, 1993. The completely revised new edition of this classic tells writers and editors what they need to know about what editors do. Articles range from "Mistah Perkins—He Dead: Publishing Today" to "Editing Crime Fiction."

Judd, Karen. *Copyediting: A Practical Guide.* 2nd ed. Los Altos, Calif.: Crisp Publications, 1990. A lively, readable copyediting manual, with lots of examples, as well as good advice and useful information for beginning and veteran editors alike.

McCormack, Thomas. *The Fiction Editor.* New York: St. Martin's Press, 1988. An original essay on the art and craft of fiction editing, which stresses the writing process itself.

O'Neill, Carol L., and Avima Ruder. *The Complete Guide to Editorial Freelancing.* New York: Harper & Row, 1979. A well-written, comprehensive overview of the business of freelancing. Still useful, though somewhat dated.

Plotnik, Arthur. *The Elements of Editing: A Modern Guide for Editors and Journalists.* New York: Macmillan, 1982. An engaging and practical guide to editing, especially of magazines. Also covers graphics, photography, libel, and copyright issues.

Stoughton, Mary. *Substance and Style: Instruction and Practice in Copyediting.* Alexandria, Va.: Editorial Experts, 1989. An excellent self-teaching manual of copyediting, with abundant examples and exercises. Includes essays on a variety of editing topics.

Wheelock, John Hall, ed. *Editor to Author: The Letters of Maxwell E. Perkins.* New York: Charles Scribner's Sons, 1950. The letters written by this renowned editor to his authors offer a lesson in tact and sensibility for any editor.

INDEXING

Collison, Robert L. *Indexing Books*. Rev. ed. Tuckahoe, N.Y.: John de Graff, 1967. A basic guide to the concepts and mechanics of book indexing.

Wellisch, Hans. *Indexing from A to Z*. New York: H. H. Wilson, 1991. Arranged by topics and designed for browsing, this lively, clear, well-written book covers all the basics. Excellent for beginning indexers as well as for authors preparing their own indexes.

PROOFREADING

Smith, Peggy. *Mark My Words: Instruction and Practice in Proofreading*. Alexandria, Va.: Editorial Experts, 1987. An excellent self-teaching proofreading manual, with numerous exercises.

Also see *Chicago Manual* ("Correcting Proofs"), along with Butcher's *Copy-editing: The Cambridge Handbook* ("Proofs") and Judd's *Copyediting: A Practical Guide* (Chapter 12). All offer thorough sections on proofreading useful for beginners.

Grammar, Style, and Usage

Hodges, John C., Mary E. Whitten, Winifred B. Horner, Suzanne S. Webb, with Robert K. Miller. *Harbrace College Handbook*. 11th ed. San Diego, Calif.: Harcourt Brace Jovanovich, 1990. A compact yet comprehensive guide for writers and editors, with abundant, specific examples. Covers grammar, punctuation, spelling, and diction. The most popular and user-friendly college text.

Bernstein, Theodore M. *The Careful Writer: A Modern Guide to English Usage*. New York: Atheneum, 1984. A balanced, commonsensical guide to English usage, with vivid and entertaining examples.

————. *Miss Thistlebottom's Hobgoblins: The Careful Writer's Guide to the Taboos, Bugbears, and Outmoded Rules of English Usage*. New York: Farrar, Straus & Giroux, 1991. The title says it all. "Miss Thistlebottom" editors are every writer's nightmare.

The Right Word at the Right Time: A Guide to the English Language and How to Use It. London: Reader's Digest Association, 1985. An accessible, well-presented guide; treats usage, words often confused, problem spellings, regional differences.

Tools of the Trade

Follett, Wilson. *Modern American Usage: A Guide.* Jacques Barzun, ed. New York: Hill & Wang, 1966. The American counterpart to Fowler (see below), though not as entertaining; Follett touches on subjects as diverse as "The Need for an Orderly Mind," the difference between "licorice" and "liquorice," and "Obsolete commas." A reference-shelf must.

Fowler, H. W. *A Dictionary of Modern English Usage.* 2nd ed. rev. and edited by Sir Ernest Gowers. Oxford: Oxford University Press, 1965. Although his advice on usage is mostly dated, Fowler is well worth reading for his charm, wit, and inimitable style. Many entries are little essays on the use of language. You'll be surprised to find you can't put the book down.

Morris, William and Mary. *Harper Dictionary of Contemporary Usage.* 2nd ed. New York: Harper & Row, 1985. This lively book on usage is a collaborative effort of more than one hundred panelists from writers and editors to poets and scientists; includes words often confused and features many current colloquialisms.

Strunk, William, Jr., and E. B. White. *The Elements of Style.* 3rd ed., with index. New York: Macmillan, 1979. What's left to say about Strunk and White? If you don't have it, get it!

Style Manuals

The Chicago Manual of Style. 14th ed., revised and expanded. Chicago: University of Chicago Press, 1993. Everything you want to know about bookmaking, including the editing process; grammar, style and usage; production and printing. The bible of the book business.

Jordan, Lewis, ed. *The New York Times Manual of Style and Usage.* New York: Quadrangle/New York Times Books, 1976. Best used for checking the spelling of names of places and people in the news.

Skillin, Marjorie, Robert M. Gay, et al. *Words into Type.* 3rd ed. Englewood Cliffs, N.J.: Prentice-Hall, 1974. Another authoritative style guide, with an extensive section on grammar and usage; well organized and illustrated.

U.S. Government Style Manual. Rev. ed. Washington: U.S. Government Printing Office, 1984. The standard style guide for writers and editors of government publications. Useful to all editors for its definitive list of government abbreviations. (Available by mail through the Government Printing Office.)

In addition to these general style guides, disciplines such as physics, medicine, biology, and mathematics have their own style conventions. Associations such as the American Institute of Physics, the American Mathematical Society, the American Medical Association, the American Psychological Association, and the Council of Biology Editors publish their own style manuals, which should be consulted by editors working in those particular fields.

Dictionaries

There are many good general dictionaries on the market, and it's difficult to recommend a single one. This is partly because each dictionary has its strengths and weaknesses. Before investing in a desk dictionary, it's worth browsing through some of the more popular ones, looking at the definitions, the illustrative examples, the notes on language usage, and—not least—the physical appearance of the dictionary, its presentation and layout. For freelancers, the choice may depend on the dictionary favored by the publisher or publishers they work for. In addition to the popular college dictionaries, we list some larger, unabridged dictionaries, available in libraries and in some editorial departments.

The American Heritage Dictionary of the English Language, 3rd ed. Boston: Houghton Mifflin, 1992. A highly regarded dictionary. This latest edition, which is attractive in appearance, with wide margins and many illustrations, contains more than 500 usage notes. New features are word histories and regional notes on American English.

The American Heritage Dictionary of the English Language: New College Edition, 2nd ed. Boston: Houghton Mifflin, 1983. A college edition of *American Heritage*; also strong on usage notes.

The Concise Oxford Dictionary of Current English. 8th ed. Edited by R. E. Allen. Oxford: Oxford University Press, 1990. A respected, easy-to-use dictionary in concise form. The first edition (1911) drew on the materials and methods of the *Oxford English Dictionary*. Note that this is a British dictionary, with British spellings and meanings of words.

Maggio, Rosalie. *Dictionary of Bias-Free Usage: A Guide to Nondiscriminatory Language*. Phoenix: Oryx Press, 1991. Newer than *The Handbook of Nonsexist Writing*. Organized alphabetically and includes ways to avoid racist and ageist as well as sexist language.

Merriam-Webster's Collegiate Dictionary. 10th ed. Springfield, Mass.: Merriam-Webster, 1993. The most recent edition calls itself the "voice of authority," and, indeed, most publishing houses follow *Merriam-Webster's* style, particularly on hyphenation, capitalization, and word division. A good guide for both beginners and seasoned editors.

Random House Dictionary of the English Language. 2nd ed. Unabridged. New York: Random House, 1987. A highly respected, readable big dictionary; more up to date than *Webster's Third*, particularly in regard to language usage.

Random House Webster's College Dictionary. New York: Random House, 1991. A user-friendly desk dictionary; of help to editors, the latest edition includes an appendix containing suggestions on ways to avoid sexist language.

Webster's New World Dictionary of American English, 3rd college ed. New York: Prentice-Hall, 1991. An up-to-date dictionary, with clear, crisp definitions; includes many American colloquialisms.

Webster's Third New International Dictionary. Unabridged. Springfield, Mass.: Merriam-Webster, 1961. Regarded by many editors as the best unabridged dictionary. Valued by editorial departments for its comprehensiveness and its authoritative voice on language usage.

Thesauruses

A thesaurus is a collection of words (the name comes from a Greek word meaning "treasure" or "storehouse") whose purpose is to help readers find the precise word they are looking for. The original thesaurus was compiled by Peter Mark Roget in the early nineteenth century, and was arranged according to broad categories, or concepts, such as space, time, intellect, affections. Today, there are a variety of thesauruses on the market (many bearing the name "Roget"), which fall into two main types: the category type originated by Roget, and the dictionary type, in which the words are arranged in alphabetical order. Some readers are more comfortable with one type, others with another. In addition, there are the computerized thesauruses included in most word processing programs, which vary both in the arrangement of the words and the information offered. For example, some include definitions, others do not.

Lutz, William D. *The Cambridge Thesaurus of American English*. New York: Cambridge University Press, 1994. An original and up-to-date collection of more than 200,000 synonyms and antonyms, compiled by a renowned expert on language use.

Random House College Thesaurus. New York: Random House, 1984. Uses the alphabetical approach; lists synonyms and related words, introducing each with a sample sentence.

Roget's International Thesaurus. 5th ed. Robert L. Chapman, ed. New York: HarperCollins, 1992. Still considered the standard; in this latest edition of the *real* Roget, words are arranged in more than a thousand categories.

Webster's New Dictionary of Synonyms. Springfield, Mass.: Merriam-Webster, 1984. Uses an alphabetical arrangement and defines each synonym, sometimes at length; with quotations from both classic and contemporary writers to illustrate the meanings of words.

Other Reference Books

Bartlett, John. *Bartlett's Familiar Quotations*. Boston: Little, Brown, 1992. The editor's first source for checking the accuracy and authorship of quotations. A key word or phrase is enough to help you locate the quotation by using the index.

Benét's Reader's Encyclopedia. 3rd ed. New York: Harper & Row,

1987. A one-volume encyclopedia of world literature, with names of writers, works, and major characters in literature, myth and legend; a useful research source.

Directory of Corporate Affiliations. Wilmette, Ill.: National Register Publishing, current edition. Gives names and locations of major U.S. corporations and their subsidiaries.

Directory of Publications Resources. Alexandria, Va.: EEI, current edition. A compendium of information (including books, computer software, organizations, contests, and tools) for publishing professionals.

Encyclopedia of Associations. Debra M. Burek, Karin E. Koek, and Annete Novallo, eds. Detroit: Gale Research, 1990. A guide to national and international organizations, public and private.

An Encyclopedia of World History. William L. Langer, ed. 5th ed. Boston: Houghton Mifflin, 1973. A chronologically arranged reference book of world history from the Paleolithic period to the present.

Gale Directory of Publications and Broadcast Media. Detroit: Gale Research, published annually. A guide to publications and broadcasting stations. Contains addresses and phone numbers.

Hammond Atlas of the World. Maplewood, N.J.: Hammond, 1992. Our first choice in an atlas.

Miller, Casey, and Kate Swift. *The Handbook of Nonsexist Writing.* 2nd ed. New York: Harper & Row, 1988. A handy guide to avoiding sexist language.

The New Columbia Encyclopedia. William H. Harris and Judith S. Levey, eds. New York: Columbia University Press, 1975. An excellent one-volume encyclopedia, with clear, well-written articles. *The Concise Columbia Encyclopedia,* 2nd ed. (New York: Columbia University Press, 1989) contains less information but is of more manageable desk size and more up to date.

New International Atlas. New York: Rand McNally, 1993. Serviceable and considerably less expensive than Hammond.

New York Public Library Book of Chronologies. Edited by Bruce Wetterau. New York: Prentice-Hall, 1990. Dates, dates, dates. A collection of timelines in fourteen broad subject categories, from "Nations and Empires" to "Accidents and Disasters" to "Sports."

New York Public Library Book of How and Where to Look It Up. Edited by Sherwood Harris. New York: Prentice-Hall, 1991. A one-volume reference guide to the most up-to-date and most readily available resources.

New York Public Library Desk Reference. New York Public Library Staff. Englewood Cliffs, N.J.: Prentice-Hall, 1989. A compilation of the information "most frequently sought" by users of the library's telephone reference services.

The Statesman's Year-Book: Statistical and Historical Annual of the States of the World. New York: St. Martin's Press, published annually. Contains political, economic, and social data about the nations of the world, as well as listings of international organizations. Invaluable for checking names of government officials, population figures, and like details.

U.S. Government Manual. Washington: U.S. Government Printing Office, published annually. The official handbook of the U.S. government; provides information on government agencies as well as on international organizations; includes lists of key government officials.

Webster's New Biographical Dictionary. Springfield, Mass.: Merriam-Webster, 1988. A single-volume reference work containing short, fact-oriented biographies of nonliving persons. Useful for checking spelling and alphabetization of personal names as well as birth and death dates.

Webster's New Geographical Dictionary. Rev. ed. Springfield, Mass.: Merriam-Webster, 1988. Quick reference for checking spelling and alphabetization of place names. Includes alternate and former names.

Whitaker's Almanack. London: J. Whitaker, published annually. The classic British almanac. Covers both British and world affairs.

Who's Who in America: A Biographical Dictionary of Notable Living Men and Women. Chicago: A. N. Marquis. Revised and reissued biennially. Lists prominent living Americans, their education and accomplishments, publications, awards, and so on. From the same publisher, there is also a *Who's Who in the World*, a *Who's Who of American Women*, as well as *Who's Whos* in specialized fields such as science, engineering, and entertainment.

The World Almanac and Book of Facts. New York: Newspaper Enterprise Association, published annually. A yearly chronology of world events, from politics to population to sports. Lists of U.S. presidents, members of Congress and the judiciary, and many other useful facts.

Many reference books are now available on CD-ROM. For example, *Microsoft Bookshelf* contains *The Concise Columbia Encyclopedia*, *The American Heritage Dictionary*, the current year's *World Almanac and Book of Facts*, and *The Concise Columbia Dictionary of Quotations*, among other titles. Reasonably priced.

Books on Writing

All the books listed here have been discussed in Chapter 5, under "Learning to Think Like a Writer."

Braine, John. *Writing a Novel*. New York: McGraw-Hill, 1975.
Dillard, Annie. *The Writing Life*. New York: HarperCollins, 1990.
Gardner, John. *The Art of Fiction: Notes on Craft for Young Writers*. New York: Random House, 1991.
Zinsser, William. *On Writing Well: An Informal Guide to Writing Nonfiction*. 4th ed. New York: HarperCollins, 1990.

Periodicals

EFA and the other freelance editorial organizations will send you a sample of their newsletter in their membership package; free samples are also available on request of *Copy Editor* and *The Editorial Eye*. You can buy a single issue of *Publishers Weekly* for a reasonable fee. For current subscription rates, please contact the publisher at the address listed below.

Active Voice (*La voix active*). Freelance Editors' Association of Canada, 35 Spadina Rd., Toronto, Ont. M5R 2S9. Monthly. Editing industry updates and news about FEAC. Advice and tips on all sorts of freelance concerns, from white-out liquid to phone services to PCs and fax machines.
Copy Editor: The National Newsletter for Professional Copy Editors. Edited by Mary Beth Protomastro. P.O. Box 604, Ansonia

Station, New York, NY 10023–0604. Bimonthly. The only publication just for copyeditors: with updates on grammar, spelling, punctuation, style and usage, and computer technology and software, as well as helpful articles ranging from choosing the right dictionary to avoiding libelous words.

The Editorial Eye. Editorial Experts, Inc., 66 Canal Center Plaza, Suite 200, Alexandria, VA 22314–1538. Monthly. For editors, writers, and publications managers. Practical information and advice on setting editorial style and managing people and schedules, with book and computer software reviews. EEI also publishes a small but excellent list of books for publications professionals.

Editorial Freelancers Association Newsletter. EFA. 71 West 23rd Street, Suite 1504, New York, NY 10010. Bimonthly. Useful articles for editors and writers on everything from marketing freelance services to ergonomics. "The Wizard of Rs" column answers questions about thorny editorial problems.

Freelance Editorial Association News. Freelance Editorial Association. P.O. Box 835, Cambridge, MA 02238. Quarterly. Informative articles on such topics as negotiating with clients, choosing a computer, setting up a freelance business, and desktop publishing.

Key Words. The American Society of Indexers, P.O. Box 386, Port Aransas, TX 78373. Issued six times per year. Regular features include "Indexing Workshop" and "Member Networking Notebook" and practical articles such as "How to Get Clients" and "Preparing Textbook Indexes."

Publishers Weekly. Published 51 times a year by R. R. Bowker. New York. The one and only. A weekly who's who and what's what in publishing, read by everyone in the industry; covers publishing people, lists job promotions and appointments as well as industry events such as book fairs; reports on new trends and new technology; reviews new books. Each issue lists staff and freelance job openings.

Electronic Sources

See Annotated Bibliography at the end of Chapter 7.

Getting the Facts by Phone

Copyeditors, particularly those who work on reference books, do a lot of fact checking, and not infrequently the information they want isn't to be found in the books they have at hand. This is particularly true when it comes to checking current or very recent data, such as the latest exchange rate of the Thai *baht* against the British pound, or a relatively obscure fact, say, the birthplace of a soccer player from Argentina. In such cases, a phone call may yield the answer in a relatively short time—provided you know where to call.

For example, most major banks will provide information on currency exchange rates. And a call to the Argentinean embassy—or the nearest consulate—would probably be the quickest way to find out that soccer player's home town or village. Embassies and consulates, which generally have a press officer or a public relations official to answer questions from writers, researchers, or the general public, are an excellent source of information on other countries. So is the U.S. State Department, which has "desks" for almost every country in the world; the experts who staff each desk are knowledgeable about the economic, political, and cultural aspects of the country in which they specialize. And for information about U.S. states, the state governor's office is often a good place to start.

When it comes to checking facts about big business, it's well to remember that all major corporations have public relations departments. That's where to go to check the name of a company executive, the company's most recent sales figures, the launch date of a new product, or the status of an ongoing labor/management dispute.

Another, often overlooked, resource is the advocacy groups, who are eager to disseminate information about the cause they are working for. The National Audubon Society or the Sierra Club may be able to provide data on the status of an endangered species or the number of oil spills in the past twelve months; a right-to-die group may know when a pending lawsuit on the issue is likely to come to court.

If you live in or near a big city, the quickest way to get an answer to a hard-to-track-down general knowledge question may be to call your public library. Many public libraries in both the United States and Canada (as well as many university libraries) have reference phones, which handle millions of calls every year.

Following is a list of library phone numbers in some major cities; if your city isn't included, check with your local library.

Library Telephone Reference Numbers

Boston: Boston Public Library	(617) 536–5400
Chicago: Chicago Public Library	(312) 269–2900
Cincinnati: Public Library of Cincinnati	
and Hamilton County	(513) 639–6900
Cleveland: Cleveland Public Library	(216) 623–2800
Dallas: Dallas Public Library	(214) 749–4100
Detroit: Detroit Public Library	(313) 833–1000
Houston: Houston Public Library	(713) 224–5441
Kansas City: Kansas City Public Library	(816) 221–2685
Los Angeles:	
Los Angeles Public Library System	(213) 612–3200
Los Angeles County Public Library System	(213) 922–8131
Milwaukee: Milwaukee Public Library	(414) 278–3000
New York:	
Brooklyn Public Library	(718) 780–7700
New York Public Library	(212) 930–0800
Queens Borough Public Library	(718) 990–0700
New York State Library (Albany)	(518) 474–5930
Philadelphia: Free Library of Philadelphia	(215) 686–5322
Pittsburgh: Carnegie Library of Pittsburgh	(412) 622–3100
Washington, D.C.: Library of Congress	(202) 287–5000

Grammar Hotlines[1]

The telephone grammar hotlines listed here are a quick, easy way for an editor to check a point of grammar, punctuation, spelling, diction, or syntax, especially when he or she is temporarily without a basic text. The hotlines are in no way meant to be a substitute for a thorough grounding in grammar or a knowledge of relevant style guides and usage manuals and how to use them.

ALABAMA

Jacksonville: Grammar Hotline—(205) 782–5409, Jacksonville State University
Tuscaloosa: Grammar Hotline—(205) 348–5049, University of Alabama

ARKANSAS

Little Rock: The Writer's Hotline—(501) 569–3477, University of Arkansas

CALIFORNIA

Moorpark: National Grammar Hotline—(805) 378–1494, Moorpark College
Sacramento: English Help Line—(916) 688–7444, Cosumnes River College

COLORADO

Pueblo: USC Grammar Hotline—(719) 549–2787, University of Southern Colorado

[1] The *Grammar Hotline Directory* is reprinted by permission of Tidewater Community College, Virginia Beach Campus, Virginia Community College System. For each free copy of the directory, send a self-addressed, stamped (first-class postage), business-letter–size envelope to Grammar Hotline Directory, Tidewater Community College Writing Center, 1700 College Crescent, Virginia Beach, VA 23456. For further information, contact Donna Reiss, Writing Center/Grammar Hotline Director, (804) 427–7170.

DELAWARE

Newark: Grammar Hotline—(302) 831–1890, University of Delaware

FLORIDA

Coral Gables: Grammar Hotline—(305) 284–2956, University of Miami

Ft. Lauderdale: Grammar Hotline—(305) 475–6596, Broward Community College, Central Campus

Pensacola: Writing Center and Grammar Hotline—(904) 474–2129, University of West Florida

GEORGIA

Atlanta: Writing Center—(404) 651–2906, Georgia State University

Rome: Grammar Hotline—(706) 295–6312, Floyd College

ILLINOIS

Charleston: Grammar Hotline—(217) 581–5929, Eastern Illinois University

Des Plaines: The Write Line: "Dr. Grammar"—(708) 635–1948, Oakton Community College

Normal: Grammar Hotline—(309) 438–2345, Illinois State University

Oglesby: Grammarline—(815) 224–2720, Illinois Valley Community College

Palatine: Grammar "Right" Line—(708) 397–3000, ext. 2389, William Rainey Harper College

River Grove: Grammarphone—(708) 456–0300, ext. 254, Triton College

INDIANA

Indianapolis: IUPUI Writing Center Hotline—(317) 274–3000, Indiana University—Purdue University at Indianapolis

Muncie: Grammar Crisis Line—(317) 285–8387, Ball State University

West Lafayette: Grammar Hotline—(317) 494–3723, Purdue University

KANSAS

Emporia: Writer's Hotline—(316) 343–5380, Emporia State University

Overland Park: Grammar Hotline—(913) 469–4413, Johnson County Community College

LOUISIANA

Lafayette: Grammar Hotline—(318) 231–5224, University of Southwestern Louisiana

MARYLAND

Baltimore: Writer's Hotline—(410) 455–3052, University of Maryland, Baltimore County

Emmitsburg: Grammar Hotline—(301) 447–5367, Mount St. Mary's College

Frostburg: Grammarphone (patented trademark)—(301) 689–4327, Frostburg State University

MASSACHUSETTS

Boston: Grammar Hotline—(617) 373–2512, Northeastern University

Lynn: Grammar Hotline—(617) 593–7284, North Shore Community College

MICHIGAN

Flint: Grammar Hotline—(313) 762–0229, C. S. Mott Community College

Kalamazoo: Writer's Hotline—(616) 387–4442, Western Michigan State University

Lansing: Writer's Hotline—(517) 483–1040, Lansing Community College

MISSOURI

Joplin: Grammar Hotline—(417) 624–0171, Missouri Southern State College

Kansas City: Writer's Hotline—(816) 235–2244, University of Missouri, Kansas City

Springfield: Writer's Hotline—(417) 836–6398, Southwest Missouri State University

St. Louis: Writer's Hotline—(314) 367–8700, ext. 244, St. Louis College of Pharmacy

NEW JERSEY

Jersey City: Grammar Hotline—(201) 200–3337 or 200–3338, Jersey City State College, Harlan Hamilton

NORTH CAROLINA

Fayetteville: Grammar Hotline—(919) 630–7000, Methodist College

Greenville: Grammar Hotline—(919) 757–6399, East Carolina University

OHIO

Ashland: Ashland University Writing Center—(419) 289–5110, Ashland University

Cincinnati: Dial-A-Grammar—(513) 745–5731, Raymond Walters College

Cincinnati: Writing Center Hotline—(513) 569–1736 or 569–1737, Cincinnati Technical College

Cleveland: Grammar Hotline—(216) 987–2050, Cuyahoga Community College

Dayton: Writer's Hotline—(513) 873–2158, Wright State University

Delaware: Writing Resource Center—(614) 368–3925, Ohio Wesleyan University

Orrville: Grammar Hotline—(216) 683–2010, University of Akron, Wayne College

OKLAHOMA

Bethany: Grammar Hotline—(405) 491–6328, Southern Nazarene University

Chickasha: Grammar Hotline—(405) 224–8622

OREGON

Portland: Writing Helpline—(503) 725–3570, Portland State University Writing Lab

PENNSYLVANIA

Allentown: Academic Support Center—(215) 437–4471, Cedar Crest College

Glen Mills: Burger Associates—(215) 399–1130

Philadelphia: Writer's Helpline—(215) 204–5612, Temple University

Pittsburgh: Grammar Hotline—(412) 344–9759, Chatham College

SOUTH CAROLINA

Charleston: Writing Hotline—(803) 953–3194, The Citadel

Columbia: Writer's Hotline—(803) 777–7020, University of South Carolina

Spartanburg: Writer's Hotline—(803) 596–9613 or 596–9186, Converse College

TEXAS

Amarillo: Grammarphone—(806) 374–4726, Amarillo College

Houston: University of Houston Downtown Grammar Line—(713) 221–8670

San Antonio: Dial-a-Tutor—(512) 733–2503, San Antonio College

VIRGINIA

Sterling: Interdisciplinary Writing Center—(703) 450–2511, Northern Virginia Community College, Loudoun Campus

Virginia Beach: Grammar Hotline—(804) 427–7170, Tidewater Community College

WEST VIRGINIA

Montgomery: Writer's Hotline—(304) 442–3119, West Virginia Institute of Technology

WISCONSIN

Platteville: Grammar Hotline—(608) 342–1615, University of Wisconsin, Platteville

Stevens Point: Writer's Hotline—(715) 346–3528, University of Wisconsin, Stevens Point Tutoring-Learning Center

CANADA

Edmonton, Alberta: Grammar Hotline—(403) 497–5663, MacEwan Community College

Publishing Courses

The following are brief descriptions of courses offered in publishing and editing. For more complete information about what's offered when, and the costs, write or phone the individual university or organization.

American Society of Indexers (ASI)
P.O. Box 386
Port Aransas, TX 78373–0386
(512) 749–4052
Sponsors seminars, workshops, and tours of professional interest throughout the year.

Arizona State University
Scholarly Publishing Program
History Department
Arizona State University
Tempe, AZ 85287–2501
(602) 965–4188
Dir.: Beth Luey
Offers graduate students the opportunity to receive training in publishing studies. Prepares them for careers with university presses, reference book publishers, commercial scholarly presses, journals, and college textbook publishers. Comprehensive courses include Research in Scholarly Publishing, Scholarly Editing, Fine Printing and Bookmaking, Censorship and Literature, and Popular Science Writing. Certificate in Scholarly Publishing.

Chicago Book Clinic
Professional Publishing Education Program
111 East Wacker Drive, Suite 200
Chicago, IL 60601
(312) 946–1700
Courses and seminars in editing and proofreading, production and design; book publishing and desktop publishing; typesetting, printing, and binding.

Columbia University, School of General Studies
The Writing Program
615 Lewisohn Hall
Columbia University
New York, NY 10027
(212) 854–3774
Dir.: Alan Ziegler
Publishing (as well as creative writing) courses include The Author and the Manuscript and Literary Editing and Publishing. For undergraduate degree candidates and nondegree students.

EEI (formerly Editorial Experts, Inc.)
Training Division
66 Canal Center Plaza, Suite 200
Alexandria, VA 22314-5507
(703) 683-7453; fax (703) 683-4915
Mgr.: Sally Smith
Provides publications professionals with the ability to make "all the right moves." Comprehensive courses (basic to advanced level) include grammar, proofreading, indexing, writing/editing, production, design, management, computer training (Macintosh and PC). Professional Sequence Certificates offered.

Editorial Freelancers Association (EFA)
71 West 23rd Street, Suite 1504
New York, NY 10010
(212) 929-5400; fax: (212) 929-5439
Career-enhancing courses for freelance and in-house editorial professionals (and writers) include: Promoting Your Business; Basic Proofreading; Introduction to Picture Research; Textbook Development; Editing Yourself for Publication.

Freelance Editors' Association of Canada (FEAC)
35 Spadina Road
Toronto, Ontario M5R 2S9
(416) 975-1379; fax: (416) 975-1839
Seminars cover a variety of topics for everyone from the novice to the experienced editor; for in-house and freelance editors.

Georgetown University, Professional Development
    Program in Editing and Publications
Professional Development Program—SSCE
Georgetown University
Washington, DC 20057
(202) 687-6218
Semester courses include principles of writing and editing; advanced editing, copyediting, and proofreading; graphic design and theory. Course-completion certificate offered.

George Washington University, The Center for Career
    Education and Workshops
2020 K Street N.W., Suite B-100
Washington, DC 20052
(202) 994-5299; fax: (202) 293-2650

Dir.: Marilyn Millstone
Publication Specialist Program and Desktop Publishing Program. Graduate-level courses and seminars for recent graduates and publishing professionals. Basic and advanced courses include: Fundamentals of Proofreading and Copyediting; Substantive Editing; Publications Management; Writing for Editors; Practical Approach to Nonprofit Publishing; Introduction to Operating Systems (IBM and Mac). Courses can be taken individually or for Publishing Specialist Certificate and Desktop Publishing Specialist Certificate.

Hofstra University, English Department
1000 Fulton Avenue
Hempstead, NY 11550
(516) 463–5454
Chairperson, English Dept.: Associate Professor
  Robert B. Sargent
Dir., Creative Writing and
  Publishing Studies Programs: Professor Julia Markus
Undergraduate courses (Creative Writing and Literature; Publishing Studies and Literature) leading to a B.A. in English. Publishing courses include: book editing, design, and production; book promotion; books and the law.

Howard University Press, Book Publishing Institute
1240 Randolph Street, N.E.
Washington, DC 20017
(202) 806–4943
Five-week (late May to early July) intensive course provides overview of the book publishing industry. Courses cover editing, design, production, and marketing. Course-completion certificate offered.

New York University Center for Publishing
School of Continuing Education
48 Cooper Square, Suite 108
New York, NY 10003
(212) 998–7219; fax: (212) 995–4131
Program Administrator: Miriam Rivera

Certificate Program in Book Publishing for "young and more experienced" publishing professionals. Fall and spring courses include Books from Reader to Writer: An Overview of the Publishing Process; Copyediting and Proofreading Fundamentals; Becoming a Book Editor; Production Editing; How to Market Your Freelance Editorial Services; Introduction to the Graphics Process. Courses can be taken individually or for certificates.

New York University Summer Institute in Book
   and Magazine Publishing
School of Continuing Education
48 Cooper Square, Suite 108
New York, NY 10003
(212) 998–7219; fax: (212) 995–4131
Program Administrator: Miriam Rivera
Intensive seven-week program for recent college graduates planning a career in publishing. First three weeks on book publishing: emphasis on the total publication process from author and editor to distribution and subsidiary rights; second three weeks on magazine publishing: emphasis on editorial and design skills; marketing, advertising, circulation, managing the total magazine. Lectures, workshops, simulations, career planning sessions, field trips. Assistance in job placement.

New York University, Gallatin Division
715 Broadway, Room 601
New York, NY 10211-0152
(212) 998–7370; fax: (212) 998–7351
Program Dir.: Albert N. Greco
MA degree with concentration in publishing studies. Graduate courses include Book Publishing; Mass Market Paperbound Book Publishing; Scholarly Book and Journal Publishing; Business Magazine Publishing; Intellectual Property Seminar; The History of the Book.

Pace University, Master of Science in Publishing
Department of English
Pace Plaza
New York, NY 10038-1502
(212) 346–1417 or 346–1416
Chairperson: Professor Sherman Raskin

Comprehensive education in all aspects of the publishing business: editorial, production, marketing, finance, acquisitions and subsidiary rights, and new technologies. Program includes a publishing internship. Thirty-six-credit program leading to M.S. degree in Publishing.

Radcliffe College/Harvard University, Radcliffe
  Publishing Course
77 Brattle Street
Cambridge, MA 02138
(617) 495–8678; fax: (617) 495–8422
Dir.: Lindy Hess
Intensive six-week course concentrates on book publishing (manuscript evaluation, editing, design, production, promotion, advertising, and marketing). Book workshop requires students to form publishing "companies." Second part of the course covers all areas of planning, writing, designing, and producing a magazine. Magazine workshop requires students to develop proposals for new magazines. Extensive job placement and support services all year.

Rice University, Publishing Program
Office of Continuing Studies and Special Programs
P.O. Box 1892
Houston, TX 77251-1892
(713) 520–6022 or 527–4803
Classes in all areas of book and magazine publishing. Continuing education and undergraduate credits offered.

Simon Fraser University, Writing and Publishing
  Program in Continuing Studies
Simon Fraser University at Harbour Centre
Writing and Publishing Program, Continuing Studies
515 West Hastings Street
Vancouver, British Columbia, Canada V6B 5K3
(604) 291–5000
Courses in publishing, editing, and proofreading as well as in desktop publishing and computer graphics. No credit offered.

Society for Scholarly Publishing (SSP)
10200 West 44th Avenue, #304
Wheat Ridge, CO 80033
(303) 422–3914

For everyone involved in the scholarly communication process. Offers seminars and workshops.

Stanford Professional Publishing Course, Stanford
  University
Stanford Alumni Association
Bowman Alumni House
Stanford, CA 94305-4005
(415) 723-0544; fax: (415) 725-8676
Dir.: Della van Heyst
An intensive 13-day course on book and magazine publishing for professionals; seminars and case studies on editorial decisions, design, marketing, sales, finance, strategic planning, law and intellectual properties, and new technologies. No credit offered.

University of California Extension Certificate
  Program in Publishing
2223 Fulton Street
Berkeley, CA 94720
(510) 642-4231; fax: (510) 643-8683
Certificate program in publishing. Courses in book and magazine publishing include Copyediting, Substantive Nonfiction Editing, Indexing, Contemporary Typography and Letterforms, Publication Design. Study Program in Copyediting also featured.

University of Chicago, Publishing Program
5835 Kimbark Avenue
Chicago, IL 60637-1608
(312) 702-1682; fax: (312) 702-6814
Dir.: Stephanie Medlock
Courses in book and magazine publishing and writing include Basic Manuscript Editing (*The Chicago Manual* is used extensively); Introduction to Book Production; Marketing in the Nineties; The Author–Editor Relationship; Copyright Issues in Publishing. Course-completion certificates offered.

University of Connecticut, Department of English
Box U-25, 337 Mansfield Rd., Room 332
Storrs, CT 06268
(203) 481-9095; 486-2141
Professor Feenie Ziner

Course provides an overview of magazine and book publishing for undergraduates interested in pursuing careers in these fields. Lectures by guest professionals cover many subject areas, including editing, production, and printing; advertising, promotion, and sales. Special projects give students hands-on experience.

University of Denver, Publishing Institute
2075 South University Boulevard., #D-114
Denver, CO 80210
(303) 871–2570; fax: (303) 871–2501
Dir.: Elizabeth A. Geiser

Concentrated four-week, full-time course devoted to book publishing. Workshops in editing, marketing, and production; lecture/teaching sessions include: Editor/Author Relations, The Role of the Literary Agent, Computer Technology/Applications to Book Publishing, Publicity, Subsidiary Rights, Paperback Publishing, Children's Book Publishing. Features a career session on magazine publishing. Career counseling offered. For six quarter hours of graduate credit.

Index

Index

Index

Index

Index